Society of Colonial Wars

History, charter and by-laws of the Society of Colonial Wars in the state of Illinois

List of officers and members

Society of Colonial Wars

History, charter and by-laws of the Society of Colonial Wars in the state of Illinois
List of officers and members

ISBN/EAN: 9783337150792

Printed in Europe, USA, Canada, Australia, Japan

Cover: Foto ©ninafisch / pixelio.de

More available books at **www.hansebooks.com**

HISTORY
CHARTER AND BY-LAWS

OF THE

SOCIETY OF COLONIAL WARS

IN THE

STATE OF ILLINOIS.

LIST OF OFFICERS AND MEMBERS.

Together with a record of the service performed by their Ancestors in the Wars of the Colonies.

PUBLICATION No. 2.

CHICAGO.
1896.

COMPILED BY

THE SECRETARY OF THE SOCIETY.

OFFICERS, 1896.

GOVERNOR
EDWARD McKINSTRY TEALL

DEPUTY-GOVERNOR
SAMUEL EBERLY GROSS

LIEUTENANT-GOVERNOR
LYMAN DRESSER HAMMOND

SECRETARY
SEYMOUR MORRIS
5342 Washington Avenue.

DEPUTY-SECRETARY
WILLIAM RUGGLES TUCKER

TREASURER
FRANK EUGENE SPOONER
849 Marquette Bldg.

REGISTRAR
JOHN SMITH SARGENT

HISTORIAN
EDWARD MILTON ADAMS

CHANCELLOR
JUDGE FRANK BAKER

CHAPLAIN
Rev. JAMES GIBSON JOHNSON, D. D.

GENTLEMEN OF THE COUNCIL
RODMAN CORSE PELL
DEMING HAVEN PRESTON
HENRY AUSTIN OSBORN
EDWARD McKINSTRY TEALL
SAMUEL EBERLY GROSS
LYMAN DRESSER HAMMOND
FRANK EUGENE SPOONER
JOHN SMITH SARGENT
EDWARD MILTON ADAMS
SEYMOUR MORRIS

OFFICERS, 1896—Continued.

COMMITTEE ON MEMBERSHIP
FREDERICK CLIFTON PIERCE
EDWARD MILTON ADAMS
SEYMOUR MORRIS

COMMITTEE ON ENTERTAINMENT
HENRY LATHROP TURNER
CHARLES THOMSON ATKINSON
JOHN CONANT LONG

DEPUTY GOVERNOR GENERAL
JOSIAH LEWIS LOMBARD

DELEGATES TO THE GENERAL COURT
HEMPSTEAD WASHBURNE
HENRY SHERMAN BOUTELL
SAMUEL EBERLY GROSS
FRANK BASSETT TOBEY
Rev. ABBOTT ELIOT KITTREDGE, D. D.

ALTERNATES
GEORGE WHITFIELD NEWCOMB
ALBERT EUGENE SNOW
EDWARD BEECHER CASE
WILLIAM WOLCOTT STRONG
CHARLES DURKEE DANA

Flag of the Society of Colonial Wars.

MEMBERSHIP.

Edward Milton Adams*
Victor Clifton Alderson
Charles Thomson Atkinson
Judge Frank Baker
Harry Jenkins Bardwell
Warren Lippitt Beckwith
Henry Sherman Boutell
George Butters
Edward Beecher Case
Chandler Pease Chapman
Charles Cromwell*
Daniel Charles Daggett
Charles Durkee Dana*
Alfred Beers Eaton
Charles Newton Fessenden
Albert Judson Fisher
Francis Porter Fisher
Wyman Kneeland Flint
James Monroe Flower
Lester Orestes Goddard
Samuel Eberly Gross*
Lemuel Ruggles Hall
Lyman Dresser Hammond*
Cyrus Austin Hardy
Maj. Forrest Henry Hathaway, U.S. A.
Rev. James Gibson Johnson, D. D.
Scott Jordan*
Rev. Abbott Eliot Kittredge, D. D.
Ebenezer Lane
Joseph Lathrop
John Larkin Lincoln, Jr.
Josiah Lewis Lombard*
John Conant Long
George Samuel Marsh

*Life Members

MEMBERSHIP—CONTINUED.

Franklin Adams Meacham
Frederick Laforrest Merrick
Anthony French Merrill
William Dorrance Messinger
Charles Kingsbury Miller*
Seymour Morris*
George Whitfield Newcomb
Henry Austin Osborn
Rodman Corse Pell*
Frederick Clifton Pierce
Charles Clarence Poole
Deming Haven Preston
Capt. Philip Reade, U. S. A.*
Charles Ridgely
Hiram Holbrook Rose
John Smith Sargent*
Albert Eugene Snow
Frank Eugene Spooner
William Wolcott Strong
Hobart C. Chatfield-Taylor
Edward McKinstry Teall*
Frank Bassett Tobey
William Ruggles Tucker*
Henry Lathrop Turner
Frederic William Upham*
Gov. William Henry Upham
John Demmon Vandercook
Horatio Loomis Wait
Hempstead Washburne*
Samuel Rogers Wells
Charles Pratt Whitney
William Ward Wight
Frederick Hampden Winston
Jonathan Edwards Woodbridge
Harry Linn Wright
Walter Channing Wyman

Society of Colonial Wars
in the State of Illinois

Banquet

Return of the Mayflower

Thursday Evening
Hotel

June 6th
1895
Metropole

LIBRARY
UNIVERSITY OF ILLINOIS
URBANA

HISTORY
OF THE
ILLINOIS SOCIETY.

On the 13th day of October, 1894, Messrs. Seymour Morris, John Smith Sargent and William Ruggles Tucker, received from the Secretary of State, at Springfield, Illinois, a charter to organize the "Society of Colonial Wars in the State of Illinois." A petition signed by sixteen gentlemen was sent to the General Society of Colonial Wars, in New York City, for the purpose of organizing a Society in Illinois. On Nov. 12, 1894, this petition was granted by the General Society, and the following gentlemen licensed to organize: Messrs. Seymour Morris, Capt. Philip Reade, U. S. A., Lieut. John T. Thompson, U. S. A., William Ruggles Tucker, John Smith Sargent, Lyman Dresser Hammond, Edward McKinstry Teall, George Francis Bissell, Frederick Hampden Winston, Edward Milton Adams, Charles Cromwell, Rodman Corse Pell, Samuel Eberly Gross, Henry Sherman Boutell, Josiah Lewis Lombard and Robert Patterson Benedict.

Messrs. Morris, Sargent and Tucker, as the three incorporators, called a meeting of the charter members at Parlor 23, Grand Pacific Hotel, Chicago, on Saturday afternoon, Dec. 7, 1894, at four o'clock, for the purpose of adopting a constitution and by-laws, election of officers and the perfection of the organization of the Society. The following gentlemen were present:—Messrs. Teall, Sargent, Winston, Bissell, Boutell, Cromwell, Lombard, Reade, Hammond, Gross, Pell and Morris.

The following officers were chosen:—Governor, Capt. Philip Reade; Deputy-Governor, Edward M. Teall; Lieutenant-Governor, Frederick H. Winston; Secretary, Seymour Morris; Treasurer, Lyman D. Hammond; Registrar, John S. Sargent; Historian, Henry S. Boutell; Gentlemen of the Council, Rodman C. Pell, Charles Cromwell, Samuel E. Gross; Committee on Membership, Edward M. Teall, Edward M. Adams and Seymour Morris.

Messrs. George F. Bissell, Rodman C. Pell and Lieut. John T. Thompson were appointed as a Committee on Entertainment.

December 19, 1894, the 219th anniversary of the Great Swamp Fight, the Society gave their first banquet at the Union League Club.

At the May Court, Mr. Boutell's resignation as Historian was accepted and Mr. Adams elected in his place.

Rev. James Gibson Johnson was elected Chaplain and Judge Frank Baker chosen Chancellor.

The Society sent a delegate to the unveiling of the monument erected by the General Society at Louisburg on June 17, 1895.

On June 6, 1895 the Society held a Banquet at the Hotel Metropole.

The Society has held four business Courts, one Special and two General Courts.

The Council has met eight times and elected to membership 75 applicants; four of whom have failed to qualify (two of said four having resigned), and death has claimed our most esteemed friend and member, Mr. George Francis Bissell.

The present active membership is seventy.

CONSTITUTION AND BY-LAWS
OF THE
ILLINOIS SOCIETY.

PREAMBLE.

Whereas, It is desirable that there should be adequate celebrations commemorative of the events of Colonial History happening from the settlement of Jamestown, Va., May 13, 1607, to the battle of Lexington, April 19, 1775;

Therefore, The Society of Colonial Wars has been instituted to perpetuate the memory of those events, and of the men who, in military, naval, and civil positions of high trust and responsibility, by their acts of counsel, assisted in the establishment, defense, and preservation of the American Colonies, and were in truth the founders of this nation. With this end in view it seeks to collect and preserve manuscripts, rolls, relics, and records; to provide suitable commemorations or memorials relating to the American colonial period, and to inspire in its members the fraternal and patriotic spirit of their forefathers, and in the community, respect and reverence for those whose public services made our freedom and unity possible.

SECTION I.
NAME OF THE SOCIETY.

The Society shall be known by the name, style, and title of "SOCIETY OF COLONIAL WARS IN THE STATE OF ILLINOIS."

SECTION II.
OFFICERS.

The officers of the Society shall be a Governor, a Deputy-Governor, a Lieutenant-Governor, a Secretary, a Deputy-Secretary, a Treasurer, a Registrar, a Historian, a Surgeon, a Chancellor, and a Chaplain; these, except the Chaplain, Chancellor, Surgeon and Deputy-Secretary, shall be *ex-officio* members and constitute the Council, with three other members elected for that purpose and chosen annually.

The officers and members of the Council and Committee on Membership shall be elected at the General Court by ballot. A plurality of the votes cast for each officer shall determine a choice thereof, and said officers and members of the Council and Committee on Membership shall hold office for the period of one year, or until their successors shall be duly elected and qualified.

SECTION III.
INITIATION FEES, DUES.

The initiation fee shall be ten dollars; the annual dues ten dollars, payable on or before the first of January of each year.

The payment at one time of fifty dollars shall exempt the member so paying from annual dues; or the payment at any one time, by a charter member, of thirty dollars, shall exempt said charter member so paying from annual dues.

SECTION IV.

GOVERNOR.

The Governor, or in his absence the Deputy-Governor, or Lieutenant-Governor, or Chairman *pro tem.*, shall preside at all Courts of the Society, and shall exercise the duties of a presiding officer under parliamentary rules, subject to an appeal to the Society. The Governor shall be a member *ex-officio* of all committees except the Nominating Committee and Committee on Membership.

He shall have power to convene the Council at his discretion, or upon the written request of two members of the Council, or upon the like request of five members of the Society.

SECTION V.

SECRETARY.

The Secretary shall conduct the general correspondence of the Society, and keep a record thereof. He shall notify all elected candidates of their admission, and perform such other duties as the Society or his office may require. He shall have charge of the seal, certificates of incorporation, by-laws, historical and other documents and records of the Society other than those required to be deposited with the Registrar, and shall affix the seal to all properly authenticated certificates of membership and transmit the same to the members to whom they may be issued. He shall notify the Registrar of all admissions to membership. He shall certify all acts of the Society, and when required authenticate them under seal. He shall have charge of printing and publications issued by the Society. He shall give due notice of the time and place of the holding of all Courts of the Society and of the

Council, and shall incorporate in said notice the names of all applicants for membership, to be voted on at said Council, and shall be present at the same. He shall keep fair and accurate records of all the proceedings and orders of the Society and of the Council, and shall give notice to each officer who may be affected by them of all votes, resolutions, and proceedings of the Society or of the Council, and at the General Court or oftener shall report the names of those candidates who have been admitted to membership and those whose resignations have been accepted, and of those members who have been expelled for cause or for failure to substantiate claim of descent. In his absence from any meeting the Deputy-Secretary shall act, or a Secretary *pro tem.* may be designated therefor.

SECTION VI.

TREASURER.

The Treasurer shall collect and keep the funds and securities of the Society, and as often as those funds shall amount to one hundred dollars, they shall be deposited in some bank in the city of Chicago, which shall be designated by the Council, to the credit of the Society of Colonial Wars in the State of Illinois, and such funds shall be drawn thence on the checks of the Treasurer for the purpose of the Society only. Out of these funds he shall pay such sums only as may be ordered by the Society or Council or his office may require. He shall keep a true account of his receipts and payments, and at each annual meeting render the same to the Society. For the faithful performance of his duty he may be required to give such security as the Society may deem proper.

SECTION VII.
REGISTRAR.

The Registrar shall receive from the Secretary and file all the proofs upon which membership has been granted, with a list of all diplomas countersigned by him, and all documents which the Society may obtain; and he, under the direction of the Council, shall make copies of such papers as the owners may not be willing to leave in the keeping of the Society.

SECTION VIII.
HISTORIAN.

The Historian shall keep a detailed record of all historical and commemoration celebrations of the Society, and he shall edit and prepare for publication such historical addresses, papers, and other documents as the Society may see fit to publish; also a necrological list of each year, with biographies of deceased members.

SECTION IX.
CHAPLAIN.

The Chaplain shall be an ordained minister of a Christian Church, and it shall be his duty to officiate when called upon by the proper officers.

SECTION X.
CHANCELLOR.

The Chancellor shall be a lawyer duly admitted to the bar, and it shall be his duty to give legal opinion on matters affecting the Society when called upon by the proper officers.

SECTION XI.
SURGEON.

The Surgeon shall be a practicing physician.

SECTION XII.
THE COUNCIL.

The Council shall have the power to call special Courts of the Society and arrange for celebrations by the Society.

The Council shall, prior to every General Court, appoint a committee of three members, exclusive of officers or members of the Council, and their report shall propose the names of candidates for the various offices.

They shall have control and management of the affairs and funds of the Society. They shall perform such duties as shall be prescribed by the Constitution and By-Laws, but they shall at no time be required to take action or contract any debt for which they shall be liable. They may accept the resignation of any member of the Society. They may meet as often as required, or at the call of the Governor. A majority shall be a quorum for the transaction of business; at the General Court they shall submit to the Society a report of their proceedings during the past year. The Council shall have the power to drop from the roll the name of any member of the Society who shall be at least two years in arrears, and shall fail on proper notice to pay the same within sixty days, and on being dropped his membership shall cease; but he may be restored to membership at any time by the Council upon his written application and the payment of all such arrears from the date when he was dropped to the date of his restoration. The Council may suspend any officer for cause, which may be reported to the Society, and action taken on the same within thirty days.

It shall be the duty of the Council to set apart,

from time to time, from the unexpended balance in the treasury, such sum or sums as the financial condition of the Society may warrant, until a sum equal to the total sum realized from life memberships shall have been so set apart.

This sum, so set apart, shall not be used for current expenses, and shall be called the "life membership fund," and may, at the discretion of the Society, be used, or invested by the Council for the Society's permanent benefit.

SECTION XIII.
VACANCIES AND TERMS OF OFFICE.

Whenever an officer of this Society shall die, resign, or neglect to serve, or be suspended, or be unable to perform his duties by reason of absence, sickness, or other cause, and whenever an office shall be vacant which the Society shall not have filled by an election, the Council shall have power to appoint a member to such office *pro tempore*, who shall act in such capacity until the Society shall elect a member to the vacant office, or until the inability due to said cause shall cease; *provided, however*, that the office of Governor or Secretary shall not be filled by the Council when there shall be a Deputy or Lieutenant-Governor, or Deputy-Secretary, to enter on the duties.

The Council may supply vacancies among its members under the same conditions, and should any member other than an officer be absent from three consecutive Councils of the same, his place may be declared vacant by the Council and filled by appointment until an election of a successor.

Subject to these provisions, all officers and gentlemen of the Council shall from the time of election continue in their respective offices until the next General Court, or until their successors are chosen.

SECTION XIV.
RESIGNATION.

No resignation of any member shall become effective unless consented to by the Council.

SECTION XV.
DISQUALIFICATIONS.

No person who may be enrolled as a member of this Society shall be permitted to continue in membership when his proofs of descent or eligibility shall be found to be defective. The Council, after thirty days' notice to such person to substantiate his claim, and upon his failure satisfactorily so to do, may require the Secretary to erase his name from the membership list. The said person shall have a right to appeal to the Society at its next Court, or at the General Court. If the said appeal be sustained by a two-thirds vote of the members present at such Court, the said person's name shall be restored to said membership list.

SECTION XVI.
QUALIFICATIONS FOR MEMBERSHIP.

Any male person above the age of twenty-one years, of good moral character and reputation, shall be eligible to membership in the Society of Colonial Wars, who is lineally descended in the male or female line from an ancestor:

(1) Who served as a military or naval officer, or as a soldier, sailor, or marine, or as a privateersman; under authority of the Colonies which afterwards formed the United States, or in the forces of

Great Britain which participated with those of the said Colonies in any wars in which the said Colonies were engaged, or in which they enrolled men, from the settlement of Jamestown, May 13, 1607, to the battle of Lexington, April 19, 1775; or

(2) Who held office in any of the Colonies between the dates above mentioned, either as

(*a*) Director-General, Vice-Director-General, in the Colony of New Netherlands;

(*b*) Governor, Lieutenant or Deputy Governor, Lord Proprietor, in the Colonies of New York, New Jersey, Virginia, Pennsylvania, and Delaware;

(*c*) Lord Proprietor, Governor, Deputy Governor, in Maryland and the Carolinas;

(*d*) Governor, Deputy Governor, Governor's Assistant in any of the New England Colonies.

SECTION XVII.
DECLARATION.

Every applicant for membership shall declare upon honor that he has not failed of admission in any other State Society and that he will use his best efforts to promote the purposes of the Society, and will observe the Constitution and By-Laws of the same.

SECTION XVIII.
ADMISSION OF MEMBERS.

Every application for membership shall be made in writing on blanks furnished by the Secretary, subscribed by the applicant, and approved by two members of the Society over their signatures. Applications shall be accompanied by proof of eligibility, and such applications and proofs shall be referred to the Committee on Membership, who shall carefully investigate the same and report at the next meeting their recommendation thereon. Members shall be elected by ballot at a Council of the Society duly called, but a negative vote of one in five of the ballots cast shall cause the rejection of such candidate. Payment of the initiation fee and dues, and subscription to the declaration contained in the By-Laws of the Society, shall be a prerequisite of membership.

After an application for membership in this Society has been accepted, if the applicant does not, within the period of ninety days after notice has been sent him, pay to the Treasurer of this Society his initiation fee and dues, and subscribe to the Constitution and By-Laws, his name shall be dropped and his application canceled.

SECTION XIX.

COMMITTEE ON MEMBERSHIP.

The Committee on Membership shall consist of three members. They shall be chosen by ballot at the General Court of the Society, and shall be elected for the period of one year. Two members shall constitute a quorum, and a negative vote of one member shall cause an adverse report to the Council on the candidate's application. The proceedings of the Committee shall be secret and confidential; and a candidate who has been rejected by the Council shall be ineligible for membership for a space of one year from date of rejection, except upon the unanimous vote of the Committee.

The Committee shall have power to make By-Laws for its government, and for other purposes not inconsistent with the Constitution or By-Laws of the Society.

SECTION XX.

EXPULSION OR SUSPENSION.

Any member for cause or conduct detrimental or antagonistic to the interest or purposes of the Society, or for just cause, may be suspended or expelled from the Society. But no member shall be expelled or suspended unless written charges be presented against such member to the Council.

The Council shall give reasonable notice of such charges, and afford such member reasonable opportunity to be heard and refute the same. The Council, after hearing such charges, may recommend to the Society the expulsion or suspension of such member, and if the recommendation of the Council be adopted by a majority vote of the members of the Society present at such Court, he shall be so expelled or suspended, and the insignia of said member shall thereupon be returned to the Treasurer of the Society, and his rights therein shall be extinguished or suspended. The Treasurer shall refund to the said member the amount paid for the said insignia.

SECTION XXI.

COURTS.

The General Court of the Society shall be held on the anniversary of the Great Swamp Fight, December 19, 1675.

Special Courts may be called by the Governor at such times as in his opinion the interests of the Society may demand, and must be called by the Secretary on the written request of three members. All notice of meetings shall be sent out at least six days before the date of the meeting.

SECTION XXII.
SERVICE OF NOTICE.

It shall be the duty of every member to inform the Secretary by written communication of his place of residence and of any change thereof, and of his post-office address. Service of any, under the Constitution or By-Laws, on any member, addressed to his last residence or post-office address, forwarded by mail, shall be efficient service of notice.

SECTION XXIII.
CERTIFICATE OF MEMBERSHIP.

Members may receive a certificate of membership, which shall be signed by the Governor, Secretary, and Registrar.

SECTION XXIV.
ALTERATION OR AMENDMENT.

No alteration or amendment of the By-Laws shall be made unless notice shall have been duly given in writing, signed by the member proposing the same, at a Court of the Society.

The Secretary shall send a printed copy of the proposed amendment to the members of the Society, and state the Court at which the same will be voted upon. No amendment or alteration shall be made unless adopted by a two-thirds vote of the members present at the Court voting upon the same.

The Society of Colonial Wars
in the State of Illinois
requests the honor of your presence
at a Banquet, to be given on
Friday, January third, 1896,
at six o'clock.

The Victoria,
Chicago.

MEMBERS
WITH THEIR LINE OF DESCENT.

MEMBERS.

No. 10   Gen. No. 828
*EDWARD MILTON ADAMS.

Tenth in descent from Gov. Thomas Dudley
Tenth in descent from William Collier.
Ninth in descent from Gov. William Leete.
Ninth in descent from Rev. John Woodbridge.
Ninth in descent from Capt. James Avery.
Ninth in descent from Gov. Thomas Prence.
Ninth in descent from Thomas Minor.
Ninth in descent from John Howland.
Ninth in descent from Thomas Stanton.
Eighth in descent from Capt. George Denison.
Eighth in descent from Lieut. John Tracy.
Eighth in descent from Capt. John Gorham.
Eighth in descent from John Griffin.
Eighth in descent from John Ruggles.

* Charter Member.

Eighth in descent from Capt. Edward Johnson.
Eighth in descent from Stephen Terry.
Seventh in descent from Lieut. Samuel Humphrey.
Seventh in descent from Sergt. John Humphrey.
Seventh in descent from Nehemiah Smith.
Seventh in descent from Nehemiah Palmer.
Seventh in descent from John Denison.
Seventh in descent from Josiah Chapin.
Seventh in descent from John Thurston.
Seventh in descent from Henry Rhoades.
Seventh in descent from Abraham Preble.
Seventh in descent from Robert Coates.
Seventh in descent from Moses Cleveland.
Seventh in descent from Lieut. David Waterbury.
Seventh in descent from Ensign John Bates, Sr.
Seventh in descent from Lieut. Joseph Kellogg.
Seventh in descent from George Denison, Jr.
Sixth in descent from Capt. Ichabod Palmer.
Sixth in descent from Lieut. Ebenezer Billings.
Sixth in descent from Joshua Holmes.
Sixth in descent from Seth Chapin.
Sixth in descent from Capt. James Lovett.
Sixth in descent from Edward Adams.
Sixth in descent from Aaron Cleveland.
Sixth in descent from Ensign Isaac How.
Sixth in descent from Lieut. Samuel Bates.
Fifth in descent from Capt. Robert Taft.
Fifth in descent from Maj. Daniel Lovett.
Fourth in descent from Samuel Rhoades.

LIBRARY
OF THE
UNIVERSITY OF ILLINOIS

LIBRARY
OF THE
UNIVERSITY OF ILLINOIS

VICTOR CLIFTON ALDERSON.

Eighth in descent from Edward Bangs.
Eighth in descent from William Collier.
Eighth in descent from Gov. Thomas Prence.
Eighth in descent from Edmund Freeman.
Seventh in descent from Robert Bartlett.
Seventh in descent from Richard Sears.
Seventh in descent from Major John Freeman.
Seventh in descent from Capt. Jonathan Sparrow.
Seventh in descent from George Williard.
Sixth in descent from Capt. Paul Sears.

No. 42   Gen. No. 1001

CHARLES THOMSON ATKINSON.

Ninth in descent from Maj. Aaron Cook.
Ninth in descent from Wm. Westwood.
Eighth in descent from Lieut. Thomas Stebbins.
Eighth in descent from Anthony Hawkins.
Eighth in descent from George Colton.
Eighth in descent from Wm. Hopkins.
Eighth in descent from Daniel Clark.
Eighth in descent from Capt. Aaron Cook.
Eighth in descent from Edward Griswold.
Eighth in descent from Edward Howell.
Eighth in descent from Maj. John Mason.
Seventh in descent from Moses Cook.
Seventh in descent from Capt. Wm. Lewis.
Seventh in descent from John Judd.
Seventh in descent from Hon. James Bishop.
Seventh in descent from Maj. John Howell.
Sixth in descent from Samuel Lewis.
Sixth in descent from Capt. Samuel Thompson.

LIBRARY
OF THE
UNIVERSITY OF ILLINOIS

No. 25   Gen. No. 897
JUDGE FRANK BAKER.

Eighth in descent from Capt. Hugh Mason.
Eighth in descent from Capt. Thomas Brooks.
Eighth in descent from Ensign James Cutler.
Seventh in descent from John Wheeler.
Seventh in descent from Sergt. Thomas Wheeler.
Seventh in descent from Lieut. Thomas Cutler.
Seventh in descent from Capt. Edward Wright.
Seventh in descent from Sergt. John Baldwin.
Seventh in descent from Capt. Thomas Topping.
Sixth in descent from Ensign Thomas Baker.
Sixth in descent from Ensign William Monroe.
Fifth in descent from Capt. Timothy Wheeler.

No. 64   Gen. No. 1059
HARRY JENKINS BARDWELL.

Seventh in descent from Sergt. Robert Bardwell.
Fifth in descent from Lieut. Ebenezer Bardwell, Jr.
Fourth in descent from Lieut. Perez Bardwell.

LIBRARY
OF THE
UNIVERSITY OF ILLINOIS

**LIBRARY
OF THE
UNIVERSITY OF ILLINOIS**

No. 75   Gen. No. 1213

WARREN LIPPITT BECKWITH.

Seventh in descent from Edward Smith.
Seventh in descent from John Whipple.
Sixth in descent from Randall Holden.
Sixth in descent from Joseph Whipple.

*GEORGE FRANCIS BISSELL.

Third in descent from Capt. Ozias Bissell.

IN MEMORIAM.

Whereas, God in his providence has removed from our midst George Francis Bissell, a Charter Member of this Society, we desire to express our sincere expressions of regret at our great loss in his death.

Mr. Bissell was born June 22, 1827, and died June 25, 1895, and had resided in this city many years, where, by his strict integrity, he had won for himself the esteem and admiration of his fellow citizens. He was a man of strong religious convictions, being at the time of his death a member and officer in the First Presbyterian Church. He was a man of marked business ability and great decision of character.

Mr. Bissell was No. 8 in the roll of membership in the Society of Colonial Wars in the State of Illinois and will be sadly missed in all our future Counsels.

Resolved, That a copy of these resolutions be spread upon the minutes of this Society and also a suitable page be placed in our year book and the same be placed in the General Societies' year book.

Resolved, That a copy be also furnished the bereaved wife and family of our lamented friend.

LIBRARY
OF THE
UNIVERSITY OF ILLINOIS

LIBRARY
OF THE
UNIVERSITY OF ILLINOIS

No. 14   Gen. No. 749

*HENRY SHERMAN BOUTELL.

Eighth in descent from Capt. John Whipple.
Eighth in descent from Capt. Timothy Wheeler.
Eighth in descent from John Prescott.
Seventh in descent from Capt. Jonathan Prescott.
Seventh in descent from Capt. John Sherman.
Seventh in descent from Edward Winship.
Seventh in descent from John Boutell.

No. 46   Gen. No. 1041

GEORGE BUTTERS.

Oak Park, Ill.

Eighth in descent from Thomas Savery.
Eighth in descent from Henry Sampson.
Eighth in descent from George Soule.
Eighth in descent from Lieut. Samuel Nash.
Eighth in descent from John Alden.
Eighth in descent from Capt. Myles Standish.
Eighth in descent from Maj. Richard Waldron.
Eighth in descent from Richard Cutt.
Seventh in descent from Samuel Harlow.
Seventh in descent from William Vaughan.
Seventh in descent from Hon. Robert Elliott.
Seventh in descent from John Gerrish.
Seventh in descent from William Butter.
Sixth in descent from Lieut. Gov. George Vaughan.
Sixth in descent from Capt. Timothy Gerrish.
Sixth in descent from George Bramhall.
Fourth in descent from Zabdiel Sampson.

LIBRARY
OF THE
UNIVERSITY OF ILLINOIS

**LIBRARY
OF THE
UNIVERSITY OF ILLINOIS**

No. 53 Gen. No. 1048

EDWARD BEECHER CASE.

Eighth in descent from John Alden.

No. 40   Gen. No. 999

CHANDLER PEASE CHAPMAN.

MADISON, WIS.

Ninth in descent from Gov. Wm. Bradford.
Eighth in descent from Major Wm. Bradford.

CHANDLER PEASE CHAPMAN.

LIBRARY
OF THE
UNIVERSITY OF ILLINOIS

No. 11   Gen. No. 746

*CHARLES CROMWELL.

Sixth in descent from Wm. Cromwell.

No. 66　　　　　　　　　　　Gen. No. 1061
DANIEL CHARLES DAGGETT.
Moline, Illinois.
Fifth in descent from Lieut. Elihu Daggett.

LIBRARY
OF THE
UNIVERSITY OF ILLINOIS

No. 30   Gen. No. 902

CHARLES DURKEE DANA.

Seventh in descent from Maj. Wm. Hathorne.
Sixth in descent from Lieut. Thomas Putnam.
Fourth in descent from Maj. Gen. Israel Putnam.

No. 23   Gen. No. 895

ALFRED BEERS EATON.

Fourth in descent from Amos Hurd.

**LIBRARY
OF THE
UNIVERSITY OF ILLINOIS**

LIBRARY
OF THE
UNIVERSITY OF ILLINOIS

No. 31   Gen. No. 903

CHARLES NEWTON FESSENDEN.

Eighth in descent from William Ward.
Seventh in descent from Lieut. Edward Woodman.
Seventh in descent from Lieut. Edward Winship.
Seventh in descent from John Ward.
Sixth in descent from John Wyeth.
Sixth in descent from Solomon Prentice.
Sixth in descent from Capt. Edward Goddard.
Fourth in descent from Philip Goodridge.
Fourth in descent from Isaac Winship.

No. 68   Gen. No. 1063

ALBERT JUDSON FISHER.

Tenth in descent from Lawrence Waters.
Ninth in descent from Capt. Walter Haines.
Ninth in descent from Henry Burt.
Ninth in descent from Commissioner Hugh Calkin.
Eighth in descent from Surveyor-Gen. John Johnson.
Eighth in descent from John Reyner.
Eighth in descent from John Moore, Sr.
Eighth in descent from John Houghton, Sr.
Eighth in descent from Jacob Farrar.
Eighth in descent from Dea. John Haynes.
Eighth in descent from John How.
Eighth in descent from John Bigelow, Sr.
Eighth in descent from Lieut. Thomas Cooper.
Eighth in descent from John Leonard.
Eighth in descent from Capt. Luke Hitchcock, Sr.
Eighth in descent from Lieut. John Steadman.
Eighth in descent from Jonathan Burt.
Eighth in descent from Dea. Samuel Chapin.
Eighth in descent from Ensign Jared Spencer.
Eighth in descent from Commissary Wm. Douglas.
Eighth in descent from Sergt. Wm. Hough.
Seventh in descent from Lieut. Wm. Avery.
Seventh in descent from Capt. Luke Hitchcock, Jr.
Seventh in descent from Major Job Lane.
Seventh in descent from Ensign John Moore.
Seventh in descent from John Houghton, Jr.
Seventh in descent from Josiah Howe, Sr.
Seventh in descent from Geo. Bennit.
Seventh in descent from John Dumbleton, Jr.
Seventh in descent from James Warriner.
Seventh in descent from Capt. Miles Morgan.
Sixth in descent from Anthony Fisher, Jr.
Sixth in descent from Capt. John Everett.
Sixth in descent from Jonathan Moore.
Sixth in descent from Henry Houghton.
Sixth in descent from Samuel Bennett.
Sixth in descent from David Morgan.

LIBRARY
OF THE
UNIVERSITY OF ILLINOIS

LIBRARY
OF THE
UNIVERSITY OF ILLINOIS

No. 45   Gen. No. 1040

FRANCIS PORTER FISHER.

Eighth in descent from Wm. Westwood.
Eighth in descent from Wm. Phelps.
Eighth in descent from Maj. Aaron Cook.
Seventh in descent from Capt. Aaron Cook.
Sixth in descent from Wm. Pitkin.
Sixth in descent from Rev. John Whiting.
Sixth in descent from John Whitney.
Sixth in descent from Lieut. George Macey.
Fifth in descent from Nathaniel Pitkin.
Fourth in descent from Capt. Moses Porter.

No. 56   Gen. No. 1051
WYMAN KNEELAND FLINT.
Milwaukee, Wis.

Sixth in descent from Lieut. John Flint.

Wyman Kneeland Flint.

LIBRARY
OF THE
UNIVERSITY OF ILLINOIS

No. 44   Gen. No. 1039

JAMES MONROE FLOWER.

Seventh in descent from Capt. Ephraim Hunt.

No. 72   Gen. No. 1210

LESTER ORESTES GODDARD.

Eighth in descent from William Spencer.
Eighth in descent from Francis Cooke.
Sixth in descent from Lieut. Samuel Humphrey.
Sixth in descent from Ensign Jacob Mitchell.
Sixth in descent from Sergt. Nathaniel Pinney.
Fourth in descent from Capt. Joseph Warner.
Fourth in descent from Ensign Jonathan Phinney.

Lester Orestes Goddard

LIBRARY
OF THE
UNIVERSITY OF ILLINOIS

S. E. Gross

No. 13   Gen. No. 748

* SAMUEL EBERLY GROSS.

Eighth in descent from Matthew Blanshan.
Eighth in descent from Sergt. Cornelius Barentsen Sleght.
Seventh in descent from Gerrit Fokar.
Seventh in descent from Louis Dubois.
Sixth in descent from Lieut. Solomon Dubois.
Sixth in descent from Abraham Dubois.

No. 24   Gen. No. 896

LEMUEL RUGGLES HALL.

Eighth in descent from James Cudworth.
Eighth in descent from Gov. Thomas Dudley.
Seventh in descent from John Ruggles.
Seventh in descent from Capt. Samuel Ruggles.
Seventh in descent from Rev. John Woodbridge
Sixth in descent from Lieut. Joseph Wheeler.
Sixth in descent from John Prescott.
Fifth in descent from Capt. Jonathan Prescott.

**LIBRARY
OF THE
UNIVERSITY OF ILLINOIS**

**LIBRARY
OF THE
UNIVERSITY OF ILLINOIS**

No. 6   Gen. No. 743

*LYMAN DRESSER HAMMOND.

Seventh in descent from Maj. Gen. Humphrey Atherton.
Seventh in descent from Lieut. John Lyman.
Sixth in descent from Lieut. Edward Morris.
Sixth in descent from James Hadlock.
Sixth in descent from Lieut. James Trowbridge.
Fifth in descent from Hon. Ebenezer Stone.
Fifth in descent from Lieut. John Dresser.
Third in descent from Lieut. Ebenezer Hammond.
Third in descent from Capt. Richard Dresser.

No. 28   Gen. No. 900

CYRUS AUSTIN HARDY.

Eighth in descent from Robert Long.
Seventh in descent from Capt. John Carter.
Seventh in descent from Lieut. James Converse.
Sixth in descent from Major James Converse.

LIBRARY
OF THE
UNIVERSITY OF ILLINOIS

**LIBRARY
OF THE
UNIVERSITY OF ILLINOIS**

No. 47   Gen. No. 1042

MAJOR FORREST HENRY HATHAWAY,
U. S. A.

Eighth in descent from Capt. Isaac Johnson.

REV. JAMES GIBSON JOHNSON, D. D.

Eighth in descent from Rev. John Mayo.
Eighth in descent from William Lumpkin.
Seventh in descent from John Alden.
Seventh in descent from Thomas Burgess.
Seventh in descent from Edward Bangs.
Seventh in descent from Samuel Mayo.
Sixth in descent from Capt. Jonathan Bangs.
Fourth in descent from Col. James Gibson.

LIBRARY
OF THE
UNIVERSITY OF ILLINOIS

LIBRARY
OF THE
UNIVERSITY OF ILLINOIS

No. 18   Gen. No. 849

SCOTT JORDAN.

Tenth in descent from Stephen Hopkins.
Ninth in descent from Nicholas Snow.
Ninth in descent from Edward Bangs.
Ninth in descent from Thomas Paine.
Ninth in descent from John Whitney.
Ninth in descent from John Doane.
Eighth in descent from Lawrence Waters.
Eighth in descent from Daniel Hudson.
Eighth in descent from Moses Cleveland.
Eighth in descent from John Bates.
Seventh in descent from Serj. Nicholas Cady.
Seventh in descent from Francis Whitmore.
Seventh in descent from Enoch Lawrence.
Seventh in descent from Josiah Cleveland.
Sixth in descent from Capt. Joseph Cady.
Sixth in descent from Ensign Thos. Whitmore.
Sixth in descent from Capt. Daniel Lawrence.
Fifth in descent from Josiah Cleveland.
Fifth in descent from Capt. David Cady.
Fifth in descent from Lieut. John Moffett.
Fifth in descent from Lieut. James McDowell.
Fourth in descent from Capt. David Cady, Jr.

No. 63   Gen. No. 1058

REV. ABBOTT ELIOT KITTREDGE, D. D.
New York City

Eighth in descent from Richard Treat.
Eighth in descent from William Collier.
Eighth in descent from Rev. John Mayo.
Eighth in descent from William Lumpkin.
Seventh in descent from Capt. Samuel Mayo.
Seventh in descent from Stephen Hopkins.
Seventh in descent from Constant Southworth.
Seventh in descent from Gov. Robert Treat.
Seventh in descent from Lieut. Wm. French.
Sixth in descent from Corporal John French.
Sixth in descent from Giles Hopkins.

LIBRARY
OF THE
UNIVERSITY OF ILLINOIS

LIBRARY
OF THE
UNIVERSITY OF ILLINOIS

No. 71   Gen. No. 1209

EBENEZER LANE.

Eighth in descent from Lieut. Thomas Leffingwell.
Eighth in descent from Lieut. Thomas Tracy.
Seventh in descent from Capt. Daniel Clarke.
Seventh in descent from Lieut. Matthew Griswold.
Seventh in descent from Ensign Thos. Leffingwell.
Sixth in descent from Ensign Thomas Lee.
Fifth in descent from Maj. Gen. Roger Wolcott.
Fourth in descent from Gov. Matthew Griswold.

No. 65   Gen. No. 1060
JOSEPH LATHROP.

Seventh in descent from Samuel Lathrop.

LIBRARY
OF THE
UNIVERSITY OF ILLINOIS

LIBRARY
OF THE
UNIVERSITY OF ILLINOIS

No. 41   Gen. No. 1000

JOHN LARKIN LINCOLN, JR.

Eighth in descent from Capt. Michael Pierce.

No. 15   Gen. No. 750

*JOSIAH LEWIS LOMBARD.

Ninth in descent from Stephen Hopkins.
Eighth in descent from Nicholas Snow.
Eighth in descent from Richard Treat.
Eighth in descent from Rev. John Mayo.
Eighth in descent from Wm. Lumpkin.
Eighth in descent from Wm. Collier.
Seventh in descent from Gov. Thomas Roberts.
Seventh in descent from Thomas Paine.
Seventh in descent from Gov. Robert Treat.
Seventh in descent from Samuel Mayo.
Seventh in descent from Constant Southworth.
Sixth in descent from James Lewis.

**LIBRARY
OF THE
UNIVERSITY OF ILLINOIS**

LIBRARY
OF THE
UNIVERSITY OF ILLINOIS

No. 60   Gen. No. 1057

JOHN CONANT LONG.

Seventh in descent from Gov. Roger **Conant.**
Seventh in descent from John Leonard.
Sixth in descent from **Capt.** Benj. Wait.

No. 39   Gen. No. 998

GEORGE SAMUEL MARSH.

Ninth in descent from Richard Carder.
Eighth in descent from Henry Burt.
Eighth in descent from Robert Bartlett.
Eighth in descent from Edward Elmer, Sr.
Eighth in descent from Rev. Samuel Skelton.
Eighth in descent from Francis Lyford.
Seventh in descent from William Carpenter.
Seventh in descent from Samuel Damon.
Seventh in descent from Shuabel Stearns.
Seventh in descent from Samuel Gorton.
Seventh in descent from Samuel Bennett.
Seventh in descent from James Sinclair.
Sixth in descent from Joseph Burt.
Sixth in descent from Samuel Bennett.
Fifth in descent from Samuel Stearns, Jr.

LIBRARY
OF THE
UNIVERSITY OF ILLINOIS

**LIBRARY
OF THE
UNIVERSITY OF ILLINOIS**

F. A. Meacham

No. 51   Gen. No. 1046

FRANKLIN ADAMS MEACHAM.
Salt Lake City, Utah.

Tenth in descent from William Collier.
Ninth in descent from John Howland.
Ninth in descent from Capt. James Avery.
Ninth in descent from Gov. Thomas Prence.
Ninth in descent from Thomas Stanton.
Ninth in descent from Lieut. Thomas Minor.
Eighth in descent from Capt. Geo. Denison.
Eighth in descent from Capt. John Gorham.
Eighth in descent from Ensign John Tracy.
Eighth in descent from Nehemiah Palmer.
Eighth in descent from Capt. Edward Johnson.
Seventh in descent from John Thurston.
Seventh in descent from Moses Cleveland.
Seventh in descent from Capt. Josiah Chapin.
Seventh in descent from Ensign John Denison.
Seventh in descent from Nehemiah Smith.
Seventh in descent from Geo. Denison, Jr.
Sixth in descent from Capt. Ichabod Palmer.
Sixth in descent from Ebenezer Billings.
Sixth in descent from Joshua Holmes.
Sixth in descent from Ensign Edward Adams.
Sixth in descent from Aaron Cleveland.
Sixth in descent from Capt. Seth Chapin.
Sixth in descent from Capt. James Lovett.
Fifth in descent from Capt. Robert Taft.
Fifth in descent from Maj. Daniel Lovett.

No. 58   Gen. No. 1053

FREDERICK LAFORREST MERRICK.

Ninth in descent from Stephen Hopkins.
Eighth in descent from Gov. Thomas Prence.
Eighth in descent from Edmund Freeman.
Eighth in descent from Nicholas Snow.
Seventh in descent from Daniel Cole.
Seventh in descent from Giles Hopkins.
Seventh in descent from Thomas Paine.
Seventh in descent from Maj. John Freeman.
Seventh in descent from William Merrick.

F. L. Merrick

LIBRARY
OF THE
UNIVERSITY OF ILLINOIS

**LIBRARY
OF THE
UNIVERSITY OF ILLINOIS**

No. 73 Gen. No. 1211

ANTHONY FRENCH MERRILL.

Seventh in descent from Lieut. Wm. French.
Seventh in descent from Capt. John Whipple.
Sixth in descent from Col. John Lane.
Sixth in descent from Jacob French.
Fifth in descent from William French.

No. 62   Gen. No. 1055

WILLIAM DORRANCE MESSINGER.

Eighth in descent from George Woodward.
Seventh in descent from Samuel Rice.
Seventh in descent from Samuel Stone.
Seventh in descent from Francis Whitmore.
Seventh in descent from Dea. John Haynes.
Sixth in descent from Thomas Blodgett.

LIBRARY
OF THE
UNIVERSITY OF ILLINOIS

No. 20   Gen. No. 892

CHARLES KINGSBURY MILLER.

Sixth in descent from Christopher Almy.

No. 20   Gen. No. 892

CHARLES KINGSBURY MILLER.

Sixth in descent from Christopher Almy.

* SEYMOUR MORRIS.

Eighth in descent from John Johnson.
Eighth in descent from John Prescott.
Eighth in descent from Robert Long.
Eighth in descent from Richard Treat.
Eighth in descent from John Bronson.
Seventh in descent from Lieut. John Hollister.
Seventh in descent from Sergt. Samuel Hickox.
Seventh in descent from Lieut. William French.
Seventh in descent from Lieut. James Converse.
Seventh in descent from Capt. John Carter.
Seventh in descent from Capt. Isaac Johnson.
Sixth in descent from Major James Converse.
Sixth in descent from Nathaniel Richardson.
Sixth in descent from Lieut. Henry Bowen.
Sixth in descent from Lieut. Edward Morris.
Sixth in descent from Capt. Richard Seymour.
Sixth in descent from Capt. Stephen Hollister.
Sixth in descent from Lieut. John Hopkins.
Sixth in descent from Capt. William Hickox.
Sixth in descent from Benjamin Graves.
Fifth in descent from Capt. Samuel Hickox.
Fifth in descent from Capt. Josiah Converse.
Fourth in descent from Lieut. Stephen Seymour.
Fourth in descent from Lieut. Edward Morris.
Fourth in descent from Lieut. Josiah Converse.

**LIBRARY
OF THE
UNIVERSITY OF ILLINOIS**

LIBRARY
OF THE
UNIVERSITY OF ILLINOIS

No. 38   Gen. No. 997

GEORGE WHITFIELD NEWCOMB.

Seventh in descent from Gov. William Bradford.
Sixth in descent from Major William Bradford.
Sixth in descent from Lieut. Andrew Newcomb.
Fifth in descent from John Cannabell.

No. 48   Gen. No. 1043

HENRY AUSTIN OSBORN.

Sixth in descent from Lieut. Cornelius Hull.
Fifth in descent from Capt. Theophilus Hull.

Henry Austin Osborn

LIBRARY
OF THE
UNIVERSITY OF ILLINOIS

LIBRARY
OF THE
UNIVERSITY OF ILLINOIS

No. 12   Gen. No. 747

* RODMAN CORSE PELL.

Seventh in descent from Major John Pell.

No. 17   Gen. No. 848

FREDERICK CLIFTON PIERCE.

Eighth in descent from Gov. Roger Conant.
Eighth in descent from John Whitney.
Seventh in descent from Ensign Edward Adams.
Seventh in descent from Lieut. Thomas Fuller.
Seventh in descent from Edward Rice.
Sixth in descent from Lot Conant, Jr.
Sixth in descent from John Green.
Fifth in descent from Zachariah Hicks.

LIBRARY
OF THE
UNIVERSITY OF ILLINOIS

LIBRARY
OF THE
UNIVERSITY OF ILLINOIS

No. 57   Gen. No. 1052

CHARLES CLARENCE POOLE.

Sixth in descent from Capt. Jonathan Poole.

No. 33   Gen. No. 992

DEMING HAVEN PRESTON.

Eighth in descent from Sergt. John Griffin.
Eighth in descent from Richard Treat.
Seventh in descent from Thomas Gridley.
Seventh in descent from Capt. Wm. Lewis.
Seventh in descent from Sergt. John Humphrey.
Sixth in descent from Lieut. Thomas Hart.

Deming Haven Preston,

**LIBRARY
OF THE
UNIVERSITY OF ILLINOIS**

Philip Reade
Capt. 3d Infantry
U.S. Army.

*CAPTAIN PHILIP READE, U. S. A.
Fort Snelling, Minn.

Ninth in descent from Sergt. John Perkins.
Eighth in descent from Corporal Thomas Barnard.
Eighth in descent from Dr. Thomas Parish.
Eighth in descent from Onesiphorus Marsh.
Eighth in descent from William Hunt.
Eighth in descent from Maj. Simon Willard.
Seventh in descent from William Sawyer.
Seventh in descent from Sergt. John Emery, Jr.
Seventh in descent from Robert Parish.
Seventh in descent from Henry Kimball.
Seventh in descent from Sergt. John Wilson.
Seventh in descent from Sergt. Thomas Flint.
Seventh in descent from Corp. Edward Coburn.
Seventh in descent from Samuel Hunt.
Seventh in descent from Lieut. Nathaniel Putnam.
Seventh in descent from Sergt. Thomas Hale.
Seventh in descent from Richard Hildreth.
Sixth in descent from Capt. Thomas Hale.
Sixth in descent from Lieut. Josiah Richardson.
Sixth in descent from Samuel Hunt, Jr.
Sixth in descent from Sergt. Samuel Wilson.
Sixth in descent from Lieut. James Hildreth.
Fifth in descent from Ephraim Hildreth.
Fourth in descent from Capt. Ezekiel Hale.

No. 70   Gen. No. 1065

CHARLES RIDGELY.

Springfield, Ill.

Seventh in descent from Lieut. Thomas Tracy.
Seventh in descent from Lieut. Thomas Leffingwell.
Seventh in descent from John Clarke.
Sixth in descent from Lieut. Solomon Tracy.
Sixth in descent from Ensign Thomas Leffingwell.
Sixth in descent from Judge Samuel Lothrop.
Sixth in descent from Lieut. Thomas Thurston.
Fifth in descent from Capt. Samuel Lothrop.
Fourth in descent from Capt. Ebenezer Lothrop.

LIBRARY
OF THE
UNIVERSITY OF ILLINOIS

LIBRARY
OF THE
UNIVERSITY OF ILLINOIS

Hiram Holbrook Rose

No. 74   Gen. No. 1212

HIRAM HOLBROOK ROSE.

Fourth in descent from Capt. Samuel Meredith.

No. 5   Gen. No. 827

* JOHN SMITH SARGENT.

Seventh in descent from Gov. Thomas Dudley.
Seventh in descent from Lieut. Thomas Putnam.
Seventh in descent from Lieut. Ralph Sprague.
Seventh in descent from John Howland.
Sixth in descent from Christopher Wheaton.
Sixth in descent from Jonathan Wade.
Sixth in descent from Capt. John Sprague.
Fifth in descent from Capt. Nathaniel Jones.
Fifth in descent from Jonathan Sprague.
Fourth in descent from Daniel Denny.

LIBRARY
OF THE
UNIVERSITY OF ILLINOIS

LIBRARY
OF THE
UNIVERSITY OF ILLINOIS

Albert Eugene Snow

No. 50   Gen. No. 1045
ALBERT EUGENE SNOW.

Ninth in descent from Edmund Freeman.
Ninth in descent from William Collier.
Ninth in descent from Stephen Hopkins.
Ninth in descent from Gov. Thomas Prence.
Eighth in descent from John Freeman.
Eighth in descent from John Jenney.
Eighth in descent from Gov. Thomas Hinckley.
Eighth in descent from Nicholas Snow.
Seventh in descent from Thomas Pope.
Seventh in descent from Thomas Huckins.
Seventh in descent from Jonathan Sparrow.
Seventh in descent from Capt. Jonathan Bangs.
Seventh in descent from Mark Snow.

FRANK EUGENE SPOONER.

Eighth in descent from John Whitney.
Sixth in descent from John Thurston.
Sixth in descent from John Ruggles.
Sixth in descent from Francis Dudley.
Sixth in descent from Josiah Chapin.
Fifth in descent from Capt. Seth Chapin.

**LIBRARY
OF THE
UNIVERSITY OF ILLINOIS**

LIBRARY
OF THE
UNIVERSITY OF ILLINOIS

No. 21   Gen. No. 893

WILLIAM WOLCOTT STRONG.

KENOSHA, WIS.

Ninth in descent from Gov. William Bradford.
Eighth in descent from Major William Bradford.
Eighth in descent from Major William Whiting.
Seventh in descent from Hon. Daniel Clark.
Seventh in descent from Thomas Burnham.
Seventh in descent from Lieut. Joseph Kellogg.
Fifth in descent from Gov. Roger Wolcott.
Fifth in descent from Ephraim Terry.
Fourth in descent from John Strong.

No. 52   Gen. No. 1047

HOBART CHATFIELD CHATFIELD-TAYLOR.

Ninth in descent from Lieut. Wm. French.
Ninth in descent from Stephen Terry.
Ninth in descent from Robert Long.
Ninth in descent from William Parks.
Eighth in descent from Richard Goodman.
Eighth in descent from Jonathan Hyde.
Eighth in descent from Capt. Isaac Williams.
Seventh in descent from John Stratton.
Seventh in descent from William Eager.
Seventh in descent from Titus Hinman.
Seventh in descent from Thomas Strong.
Sixth in descent from Francis Stiles.
Sixth in descent from Andrew Hinman.
Fifth in descent from Lieut. John Chatfield.
Fourth in descent from Asa Taylor, Sr.

LIBRARY
OF THE
UNIVERSITY OF ILLINOIS

LIBRARY
OF THE
UNIVERSITY OF ILLINOIS

No. 7   Gen. No. 744

* EDWARD McKINSTRY TEALL.

Eighth in descent from Gov. William Pynchon.
Seventh in descent from Capt. Richard Lord.
Sixth in descent from Rev. Gershom Bulkley.
Sixth in descent from Arthur Perry.
Sixth in descent from Stephen Paine.
Fifth in descent from Lieut. Richard Lord.
Third in descent from Surgeon Oliver Teall.
Third in descent from Brinton Paine.

FRANK BASSETT TOBEY.

Seventh in descent from William Swift.
Seventh in descent from Samuel Hinckley.
Seventh in descent from Andrew Hallett.
Seventh in descent from William Bassett.
Seventh in descent from Richard Sears.
Seventh in descent from Thomas Howes, Sr.
Seventh in descent from Edward Bangs.
Seventh in descent from Robert Paddock.
Sixth in descent from Thomas Howes, Jr.
Sixth in descent from James Skiff.
Sixth in descent from William Bassett.
Sixth in descent from Rev. John Smith.
Sixth in descent from Richard Bourne.
Fifth in descent from William Bassett.
Fifth in descent from Thomas Tobey, Sr.
Third in descent from Elisha Bassett.

LIBRARY
OF THE
UNIVERSITY OF ILLINOIS

LIBRARY
OF THE
UNIVERSITY OF ILLINOIS

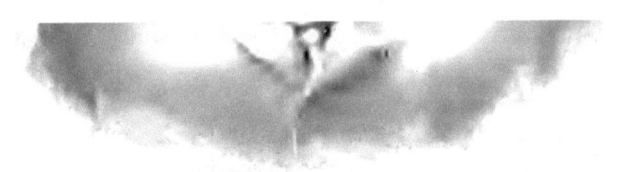

William Ruggles Fuller

*WILLIAM RUGGLES TUCKER.

Tenth in descent from John Alden.
Tenth in descent from John Paebodie.
Ninth in descent from Governor Wm. Bradford.
Ninth in descent from Gov. Thomas Dudley.
Ninth in descent from William Blake.
Ninth in descent from Andrew Hallett.
Ninth in descent from Sergt. Samuel Wilbour.
Ninth in descent from John Rogers.
Ninth in descent from John Gilbert.
Eighth in descent from Rev. John Woodbridge.
Eighth in descent from James Skiff.
Eighth in descent from Richard Bourne.
Eighth in descent from Maj. Wm. Bradford.
Eighth in descent from John Howland.
Eighth in descent from Capt. Samuel Ruggles.
Eighth in descent from John Whitcomb.
Eighth in descent from Lawrence Waters.
Eighth in descent from Daniel Warren.
Seventh in descent from Capt. Philip Pieterse Schuyler.
Seventh in descent from Oloff Stevensen Van Cortlandt.
Seventh in descent from John Hastings.
Sixth in descent from Col. Stephanes Van Cortlandt.
Sixth in descent from Samuel Farnsworth.
Fifth in descent from Brig. Gen'l Timothy Ruggles.
Fifth in descent from Lieut. David Farnsworth.
Fifth in descent from Andrew Johnstone.
Fifth in descent from Capt. Moses Tucker.

No. 36   Gen. No. 995
HENRY LATHROP TURNER.
Seventh in descent from Jonathan Gilbert.

LIBRARY
OF THE
UNIVERSITY OF ILLINOIS

LIBRARY
OF THE
UNIVERSITY OF ILLINOIS

No. 29   Gen. No. 901

FREDERIC WILLIAM UPHAM.

Seventh in descent from Lieut. Phineas Upham.

No. 55   Gen. No. 1050

GOV. WILLIAM HENRY UPHAM.
MADISON, WIS.

Sixth in descent from Lieut. Phineas Upham.

No. 67   Gen. No. 1062
JOHN DEMMON VANDERCOOK.

Eighth in descent from Samuel Eddy.
Seventh in descent from Daniel Warren.
Seventh in descent from Lawrence Waters.
Seventh in descent from John Whitcomb.
Seventh in descent from Lieut. Job Winslow.
Sixth in descent from John Hastings.
Fourth in descent from Stephen Farnsworth.

No. 26   Gen. No. 898

HORATIO LOOMIS WAIT.

Seventh in descent from John Lakin.
Seventh in descent from John Whitcomb.
Seventh in descent from Lawrence Waters.
Seventh in descent from John Whitney.
Seventh in descent from Maj. Simon Willard.
Third in descent from Capt. Joseph Wait.

**LIBRARY
OF THE
UNIVERSITY OF ILLINOIS**

LIBRARY
OF THE
UNIVERSITY OF ILLINOIS

HEMPSTEAD WASHBURNE.

inth in descent from Francis Cooke.
venth in descent from John Washburn.

No. 69   Gen. No 1064

SAMUEL ROGERS WELLS.

Eighth in descent from Gov. Thomas Wells.

**LIBRARY
OF THE
UNIVERSITY OF ILLINOIS**

**LIBRARY
OF THE
UNIVERSITY OF ILLINOIS**

No. 59   Gen. No. 1054
CHARLES PRATT WHITNEY.

Eighth in descent from Capt. Nathaniel Merriman.
Eighth in descent from Capt. William Lewis.
Seventh in descent from John Whitney.
Seventh in descent from Lieut. Samuel Ufford.
Sixth in descent from Capt. Elnathan Beach.
Sixth in descent from Capt. Samuel Cook.
Fifth in descent from Capt. Thaddeus Cook.

No. 54   Gen. No. 1049

WILLIAM WARD WIGHT.
Milwaukee, Wis.

Ninth in descent from Gov. Thomas Dudley.
Ninth in descent from Matthew Allyn.
Eighth in descent from Capt. Benjamin Newberry.
Eighth in descent from Maj. Gen'l. Daniel Denison.
Eighth in descent from Dep. Gov. Samuel Symonds.
Seventh in descent from Capt. George Barbour.
Seventh in descent from Lieut. John Lyman.
Eighth in descent from Richard Saltonstall.
Seventh in descent from Lieut. John Moseley.

**LIBRARY
OF THE
UNIVERSITY OF ILLINOIS**

LIBRARY
OF THE
UNIVERSITY OF ILLINOIS

No. 9   Gen. No. 829
   *FREDERICK HAMPDEN WINSTON.

Fourth in descent from John Mohr McIntosh.

No. 19   Gen. No. 850
JONATHAN EDWARDS WOODBRIDGE.
Eighth in descent from Gov. Thomas Dudley.

**LIBRARY
OF THE
UNIVERSITY OF ILLINOIS**

LIBRARY
OF THE
UNIVERSITY OF ILLINOIS

No. 43 Gen. No. 1038

HARRY LINN WRIGHT.

Eighth in descent from John Bronson.
Eighth in descent from Rev. Samuel Stone.
Eighth in descent from Maj. Gen'l Robt. Sedgwick.
Eighth in descent from Richard Treat.
Eighth in descent from Gov. John Webster.
Eighth in descent from William Westwood.
Eighth in descent from Maj. Aaron Cooke.
Eighth in descent from Capt. Nathaniel Turner.
Seventh in descent from Lieut. Joseph Kellogg.
Seventh in descent from Lieut. Robert Webster.
Seventh in descent from Capt. Aaron Cooke.
Seventh in descent from Stephen Terry.
Sixth in descent from Lieut. Thomas Hovey.
Sixth in descent from Capt. Joseph Wadsworth.

WALTER CHANNING WYMAN.

Seventh in descent from Lieut. John Wyman.
Sixth in descent from John Wyman, Jr.

LIBRARY
OF THE
UNIVERSITY OF ILLINOIS

ANCESTORS OF MEMBERS.

ANCESTORS OF MEMBERS.

ENSIGN EDWARD ADAMS.—Was Ensign at Medfield, Mass., 1681-1702; Deputy to the General Court many years.

REFERENCE: Society of Colonial Wars Year Book, 1895, p. 191. Tilden's History of Medfield, Mass.

   10. Edward Milton Adams.
   17. Frederick Clifton Pierce.
   51. Franklin Adams Meacham.

JOHN ALDEN.—[1599-1687]—One of the signers of the original "Mayflower Compact." Member under arms of Captain Myles Standish's Duxbury Company, 1643; assistant to all the governors of the Colony, 1633 to 1641, and from 1650 to 1686; representative to the General Court 1641-1649; member of the Council of War 1653-1660 and 1675-1676.

REFERENCE: Society of Colonial Wars Year Book, p. 48. Plymouth Colony Records; Davis Landmarks of Plymouth, p. 4.

   4. William Ruggles Tucker.
   32. Rev. James Gibson Johnson.
   46. George Butters.
   53. Edward Beecher Case.

MATTHEW ALLYN.—[—— -1671]—Windsor. Deputy to Massachusetts General Court, 1636; deputy to Connecticut General Court, 1648-1657; assistant, 1658-1667; commissioner for United Colonies, 1660-1664.

REFERENCE: Society of Colonial Wars Year Book, 1895, p. 192.

   54. William Ward Wight.

CHRISTOPHER ALMY.—In 1690 he was deputy to the General Court from Portsmouth, R. I., and the same year chosen assistant. Feb. 27, 1690, chosen or elected governor, but refused to serve for reasons satisfactory to the assembly; Aug., 1693, messenger to England from Rhode Island.

REFERENCE: Austin's Genealogical Dictionary of Rhode Island; Church's History.

   20. Charles Kingsbury Miller.

MAJOR-GENERAL HUMPHREY ATHERTON.— [——1661]—Deputy from Dorchester to the General Court, 1638, and nine times thereafter; speaker, 1653; assistant, 1654 to 1661; lieutenant, 1645; captain, 1646; commander of the Ancient and Honorable Artillery Company, 1650; commanded expedition against Pesacus, a Narragansett chief, 1650; major-general, 1661.

REFERENCE: Savage's Genealogical Dictionary of New England. Society of Colonial Wars Year Book, 1895, p. 194.

   6. Lyman Dresser Hammond.

CAPTAIN JAMES AVERY.—Commanded "100 dragoons" raised near New London, 1673, to fight against Indians; was commander of a company of 40 whites, besides about 100 friendly Indians at the Swamp fight, 1675; was one of the captors of Canonchet, 1676; was twelve times deputy to legislature, 1658-1680.

REFERENCE: Savage's Genealogical Dictionary; Conn. Colonial Records.

  10. Edward Milton Adams.
  51. Franklin Adams Meacham.

LIEUTENANT WILLIAM AVERY.—[1622-1687]—Dedham, Mass.; physician; member of Ancient and Honorable Artillery Company in 1654; representative to the General Court for Springfield, 1669; lieutenant of Dedham Military Company, 1673.

REFERENCE: Society of Colonial Wars Year Book; Savage's Genealogical Dictionary; Whitman's History of Ancient and Honorable Artillery Co., p. 164; Dedham, Mass., Town Records; Lane family, p. 17.

  68. Albert Judson Fisher.
  70. Charles Ridgely.

ENSIGN JOHN BAGG.—[1665-1740]—For many years sergeant of the military company of Springfield, Mass., and its Ensign in 1738.

REFERENCE: N. E. Hist. and Gen. Register, Vol. 29, p. 288; "West Springfield Centennial," p. 109; History of Springfield by M. A. Greene, p. 220.

  68. Albert Judson Fisher.

THOMAS BAKER.—[1618-1700]—Ensign of East Hampton, (Conn.) Company, 1654; assistant, 1658-1663.

REFERENCE: Palfrey's New England, Vol. 2, p. 638; East Hampton Records, Vol. 1, p. 58.

  25. Frank Baker.

SERGEANT JOHN BALDWIN.—Sergeant of Milford (Conn.) Militia, 1658.

REFERENCE: New Haven Historical Collection, p. 263-7.

25. Frank Baker.

EDWARD BANGS.—[1592-1678]—Of Plymouth and Eastham, Mass.; overseer or captain of the Guard against the Indians; a member of the Plymouth Military Company, 1643.

REFERENCE: N. E. Hist. and Gen. Register, Vol. 8, p. 368; Pierce's Colonial Lists, p. 76.

18. Scott Jordan.
32. Rev. James Gibson Johnson.
37. Frank Bassett Tobey.
61. Victor Clifton Alderson.

JONATHAN BANGS.—Of Eastham, Mass., was constable, 1672; selectman, 1674-1676, and later; was Ensign at Eastham, 1680, and also Ensign again, appointed Oct. 2, 1689.

REFERENCE: Plymouth Colonial Records, Vol. 5, p. 167; Vol. 6, p. 40, 218.

32. Rev. James Gibson Johnson.
50. Albert Eugene Snow.

CAPTAIN GEORGE BARBOUR.—Of Dedham and Medfield, Mass. Was a member of the Ancient and Honorable Artillery Co., 1646, was chief military officer of Medfield after 1649; defended Medfield in King Philip's War, 1675-6, and fought against the Indians at Seekouk and Rehoboth, 1676.

REFERENCE: Tilden's Medfield, 312, 87, 90; N. E. Hist. and Gen. Reg., Vol. 1, 184.

54. William Ward Wight.

LIEUT. EBENEZER BARDWELL, JR.—Of Hatfield, Mass., a member of Ephraim Williams' Company on Dec. 19, 1747; Ensign in Capt. John Ball's Company at Ft. William Henry, Oct. 11, 1756; Second Lieutenant in Capt. John Burke's Company; enlisted March 21, 1759; served until Nov. 30, 1759; Lieutenant Captain Moses Porter's Company in expedition to Crown Point.

REFERENCE: Mass. Archives, Vol. 96, p. 40.

64. Harry Jenkins Bardwell.

LIEUTENANT PEREZ BARDWELL.—Of Hatfield, Mass., a member of Capt. William Shepard's Company, June 24 to Dec. 4, 1761; a member of Capt. Salah Barnard's Company, enlisted March 5, 1760, until Oct. 5, promoted to Corporal Oct. 6, serving until Nov. 30, 1760.

REFERENCE: Mass. Archives, Vols. 96, p. 40; 99, p. 134.

64. Harry Jenkins Bardwell.

SERGEANT ROBERT BARDWELL.—Robert Bardwell was a private or trooper under Lieut. Phineas Upham; was made Sergeant and given command of the Hadley and Hatfield garrisons, leading them in the "Falls Fight."

REFERENCE: Mass. Archives, Vol. 68, p. 212; Vol. 114, p. 610.

64. Harry Jenkins Bardwell.

CORPORAL THOMAS BARNARD.—Of Salisbury and Amesbury, Mass., was a soldier in King Philip's War, 1675-77; a corporal in Capt. Wm. Turner's troop of Dorchester, Boston and Charlestown.

REFERENCE: Bodge's Soldiers in King Philip's War, p. 193-205; Mass. Archives, Vol. 68, p. 228; Savage's, Vol. 1, p. 120; N. E. H. and G. R., Vol. 6, p. 207.

2. Captain Philip Reade.

ROBERT BARTLETT.—[1603-1676].—Served in Capt. Myles Standish Company, 1632.

REFERENCE: Society of Colonial Wars Year Book, 1895, p. 196; Pierce's Colonial Lists.

39. George Samuel Marsh.
61. Victor Clifton Alderson.

ELISHA BASSETT.—Was captain at Sandwich, Mass. He held commission under Royal Governors Shirley, Pownal, Dudley and Hutchinson.

REFERENCE: Freeman's History of Cape Cod, Vol. 1, p. 335.

37. Frank Bassett Tobey.

WILLIAM BASSETT.—Was member of Capt. Myles Standish's Military Company at Duxbury, Mass., Aug., 1643.

REFERENCE: Pierce's Colonial Lists, p. 75.

37. Frank Bassett Tobey.

WILLIAM BASSETT, JR.—Was a member of Capt. Myles Standish's Military Company at Duxbury, Mass., Aug., 1643.

REFERENCE: Pierce's Colonial Lists.

37. Frank Bassett Tobey.

WILLIAM BASSETT.—Was Chief Marshal of Plymouth Colony, 1689 to 1692; was also captain at Sandwich, Mass. Representative.
REFERENCE: Pierce's Colonial Lists, p. 5; Plymouth Colonial Records, Vol. 6, p. 205, 1670-1721. Society of Colonial Wars Year Book, 1895.

37. Frank Bassett Tobey.

JOHN BATES.—[1642-1716]—Of Chelmsford. A soldier in Capt. Thomas Wheeler's Company, King Philip's War, 1675-6; also in Chelmsford Garrison, 1691-2.
REFERENCE: N. E. Hist. and Gen. Reg., Vol. 38, p. 40; Vol. 43, p. 264 and 373.

18. Scott Jordan.

JOHN BATES, SR.—Was appointed Ensign of train band at Stamford, Conn., Oct., 1685; was deputy to General Court, 1689-90.
REFERENCE: Connecticut Colonial Records, Vol. 2, p. 183; Vol. 4, p. 3.

10. Edward Milton Adams.

SAMUEL BATES.—Was appointed lieutenant of 2d Company or Train Band at Stamford, Conn., May, 1730.
REFERENCE: Connecticut Colonial Records, p. 274.

10. Edward Milton Adams.

ELNATHAN BEACH.—Was commissioned Ensign at Wallingford, Conn., Oct., 1733; lieutenant, Oct., 1740; captain, Oct., 1741.
REFERENCE: Connecticut Colonial Records, Vol. 1726-1735, p. 474; Vol. 1735-1743, p. 342-418.

59. Charles Pratt Whitney.

SAMUEL BENNETT.—[1665-1742]—Lancaster and Shrewsbury, Mass. Soldier in Queen Anne's War at Lancaster in 1704, in the garrison commanded by Ensign Peter Josslin. Was commander of garrison in 1711.
REFERENCE: Marvin's "History of Lancaster, Mass.," p. 110; Mass. Archives, Vol. 71, p. 876.

68. Albert Judson Fisher.

SAMUEL BENNETT.—[——1684]—Of Providence and East Greenwich, R. I.; in 1652 chosen general sergeant. In 1655, freeman. Oct. 27, 1656, he was ordered paid £20 for his services as sergeant; 1668-74-78, deputy to the General Court.
REFERENCE: Austin's Genealogical Dictionary of Rhode Island.

39. George Samuel Marsh.

SAMUEL (2) BENNETT.—Of East Greenwich and Coventry, R. I.; 1685, a freeman. In 1690 deputy to the General Court and a Lieutenant.

REFERENCE: Austin's Genealogical Dictionary of Rhode Island.

39. George Samuel Marsh.

GEORGE BENNIT.—Killed by Indians in the Lancaster, Mass., massacre, led by Monaco, "One-eyed John," Sunday, Aug. 22, 1675, during King Philip's War.

REFERENCE: Nourse's "Early Records of Lancaster, Mass.," p. 30, 98, 99, 252, 306, 314, 320; Marvin's "History of Lancaster, Mass.," p. 61-101.

68. Albert Judson Fisher.

JOHN BIGELOW.—[1617-1703]—Watertown, Mass. Soldier in the Pequot War and in King Philip's War. His son, John, Jr., was taken captive by the Indians at Lancaster, Oct. 15, 1705.

REFERENCE: Society of Colonial Wars Year Book; Hudson's "History of Marlborough," p. 325; Hudson's "Annals of Sudbury, Wayland and Maynard," p. 232, Ed., 1891; Bond's "Watertown," p. 29; N. E. Hist. and Gen. Register.

68. Albert Judson Fisher.

EBENEZER BILLINGS.—Of Stonington, Conn., was Ensign, Oct. 12, 1721; Lieutenant, Oct. 14, 1731, in Colonial forces.

REFERENCE: Connecticut Colonial Records, 1717-25, p. 275; 1726-1731, p. 349.

10. Edward Milton Adams.
51. Franklin Adams Meacham.

HON. JAMES BISHOP.—Secretary of New Haven Colony, 1661-1665; assistant, Conn. Colony, 1668-83; deputy governor, 1683-91.

REFERENCE: Colonial Wars Year Book, 1894; Savage's Genealogical Dictionary.

42. Charles Thomson Atkinson.

CAPTAIN OZIAS BISSELL.—Served during six years in the French and Indian War. Was in an engagement on Lake George in 1755. Was taken prisoner to Havana in 1762, where he was imprisoned for nearly nine months.

REFERENCE: Stiles History Ancient Windsor, Vol. 2, p. 103.

8. George Francis Bissell.

WILLIAM BLAKE.—[—— 1663]—Of Dorchester, Mass.; a member of the Ancient and Honorable Artillery Company of Boston.

REFERENCE: Savage's Genealogical Dictionary.

    4. William Ruggles Tucker.

MATTHEW BLANSHAN.—Early settler and land patentee at Esopus (near present Kingston) N. Y. His daughter, Katherine DuBois, wife of Louis, with her three children, another daughter, Maria Chrispel and her child, and his two younger children, were all carried into captivity at the Indian attack upon the village, June 7, 1663. He joined a rescuing expedition led by Louis Du Bois, which defeated the savages and recovered most of the captives. Member of the Hurley Military Company commanded by Capt. Paulding, stationed at Marbleton, Muster Roll dated April 4, 1670.

REFERENCE: Brodhead's History of New York, Vol. 2, p. 311-312; New York Historical Documents (Colonial Archives), Vol. 13, p. 246, 448, 449.

    13. Samuel Eberly Gross.

THOMAS BLODGETT.—Of Woburn, Mass., was private in the West Middlesex Regt. of Mass. Bay Troops; was in the garrison having headquarters at Chelmsford, his rendezvous being the garrison house of John Spaulding on March 6, 1692.

REFERENCE: N. E. Hist. and Gen. Reg., Vol, 43, p. 374.

    62. William Dorrance Messinger.

RICHARD BOURNE.—Was a member of Council of War for town of Sandwich, Mass., Feb. 29, 1675.

REFERENCE: Pierce's Colonial Lists, p. 98.

    4. William Ruggles Tucker.
    37. Frank Bassett Tobey.

JOHN BOUTELL.—Was one of the soldiers in the Reading, Mass. Co. in the Narragansett War. A private in Captain Joseph Gardiner's Company.

REFERENCE: New England Historical and Genealogical Register, Vol. 39, p. 175-177.

    14. Henry Sherman Boutell.

LIEUTENANT HENRY BOWEN.—[1633-1723]—Of Roxbury, Mass., and Woodstock, Conn., under Captain Isaac Johnson in Great Swamp fight.

REFERENCE: Society of Colonial Wars Year Book, 1894, p. 39; N. E. H. and G. Register, Vol. 39, pp. 74-78.

    1. Seymour Morris.

SOCIETY OF COLONIAL WARS

GOVERNOR WILLIAM BRADFORD.—[1589-1657]—Governor of Plymouth Colony, 1621, 1632, 1637, 1639-1643, 1648-1656. Came over in Mayflower, and was one of the signers of the Compact.

REFERENCE: Savage's Genealogical Dictionary; Plymouth Colony Records; Society of Colonial Wars Year Book, 1894; Davis' Ancient Landmarks of Plymouth.

   4. William Ruggles Tucker.
  21. William Wolcott Strong.
  38. George Whitfield Newcomb.
  40. Chandler Pease Chapman.

MAJOR WILLIAM BRADFORD.—[1624-1704]—Commanded the expedition for relief of Swanzey, June 28, 1675. Wounded by Indians in "Ye Greate Swamp Fight" Dec. 19, 1675. Deputy Governor of Plymouth, 1682-1686.

REFERENCE—Palfrey's History of New England, Vol. 2, p. 131, 148, 387, 408; Year Book, Society of Colonial Wars, 1894; Davis' Ancient Landmarks of Plymouth; Savage.

   4. William Ruggles Tucker.
  21. William Wolcott Strong.
  38. George Whitfield Newcomb.
  40. Chandler Pease Chapman.

GEORGE BRAMHALL.—Killed by the Indians in the fight at Falmouth, Me., Sept. 21, 1689.

REFERENCE: History of Portland, p. 284; Davis' Landmarks of Plymouth, p. 40.

  46. George Butters.

JOHN BRONSON.—[—— 1680]—Of Hartford, Conn.; deputy to the General Court; soldier in the Pequot battle of 1637. Took part in the Fort fight.

REFERENCE: Society of Colonial Wars Year Book, 1894, p. 47.

   1. Seymour Morris.
  43. Harry Linn Wright.

CAPTAIN THOMAS BROOKS.—[—— 1667]—Concord, Mass.; deputy to the General Court seven times, 1642-1660; Captain Concord Militia.

REFERENCE: Society of Colonial Wars Year Book, 1894.

  25. Frank Baker.

REVEREND GERSHOM BULKELEY, M. D.—[1636-1713]—Was Chaplain and Surgeon to the Connecticut Troops in King Philip's War.

REFERENCE: Society of Colonial Wars Year Book, 1895, p. 205, appendix page 17.

   7. Edward McKinstry Teall.

THOMAS BURGESS.—A private in the Sandwich, Mass. Company, 1643.
REFERENCE: Pierce's Colonial Lists, p. 73.
32. Rev. James Gibson Johnson.

THOMAS BURNHAM.—[1617-1688]—Soldier in King Philip's War.
REFERENCE: Stiles History of Windsor, Vol. 1, p. 227.
21. William Wolcott Strong.

HENRY BURT.—Of Dorchester and Springfield, Mass. Member of the first Military Company of Springfield. In 1657 he was clerk of the Train Band.
REFERENCE: Mass. Bay Colonial Records, Vol. 4, part 1, p. 314; Savage's Genealogical Dictionary.
39. George Samuel Marsh.
68. Albert Judson Fisher.

JONATHAN BURT.—At the time of the burning of Springfield, Mass., by the Indians, Oct. 5, 1675, during King Philip's War, was one of those who defended the town.
REFERENCE: Longmeadow Centennial, p. 305, appendix, p. 7; Morris' Historic Address, "The Burning of Springfield," p. 35; Mason A. Greene's History of Springfield; Geo. Bliss' Address in Chapin Family History, p. 280.
68. Albert Judson Fisher.

JOSEPH BURT.—[1673-1759]—A member of the force in garrison at Northfield in Capt. Joseph Kellogg's Co. from Nov. 20, 1723, to May 20, 1724; also in the Crown Point Expedition.
REFERENCE: N. E. Hist. and G. R.
39. George Samuel Marsh.

WILLIAM BUTTER.—Of Woburn, Mass. Private in Captain Joseph Eyll's Company at capture of 300 Indians at Checheco (Dover), Sept. 4, 1676.
REFERENCE: N. E. Hist. and Gen. Register, Vol. 41, p. 409; Savage's Genealogical Dictionary; Sewell's History of Woburn.
46. George Butters.

CAPTAIN DAVID CADY, JR.—[1742-1807]—May, 1774, commissioned Ensign of the 12th Company or Train Band of the 11th Conn. Regiment; May, 1774, Captain of the 4th Company, 11th Regiment; Captain of the 9th Company, 21st Regiment, March, 1775.
REFERENCE: Colonial Records of Connecticut, Vol. 14, p. 263, 290, 398.
18. Scott Jordan.

CAPTAIN DAVID CADY.—[1703]—Of Killingly, Conn. Oct., 1747, was commissioned captain of the 1st Company or Train Band of Killingly.

REFERENCE: Connecticut Colonial Records, Vol. 9, p. 320.

18. Scott Jordan.

CAPTAIN JOSEPH CADY.—[1666-1742]—Of Groton, Mass., and Killingly, Conn. In garrison at Groton, Mass., 1791-2. Commissioned Lieutenant of the Train Band, Killingly, Conn., Oct., 1708; commissioned Captain of the Train Band of Killingly, May, 1721; was the first Captain of the town of Killingly; Deputy to General Assembly from Killingly, 1731-33-34 and 1739.

REFERENCE: N. E. Hist. and Gen. Reg., Vol. 43, p. 373; Connecticut Colonial Records, Vol. 5, p. 75; Vol. 6, p. 239.

18. Scott Jordan.

NICHOLAS CADY.—Of Watertown and Groton. A member of Capt. Mason's Watertown Train Band, 1653.

REFERENCE: N. E. Hist. and Gen. Reg., Vol. 34, p. 281.

18. Scott Jordan.

HUGH CALKIN.—[1600-1690]—Gloucester and Lynn, Mass., and New London and Norwich, Conn. Town Clerk and Representative to the General Court for Gloucester, 1650-1651. Representative for Norwich, 1663-64. Representative for New London, 1665, and after. Was appointed Commissioner for enlisting men for an expedition against the Indians on May 21, 1653; and on Oct. 3, 1654.

REFERENCE: Savage's Gen. Dict. of N. E.; Year Book Society of Colonial Wars, 1895; Mass. Bay Colonial Records, Vol. 2, p. 98; Vol. 4, part 1, pp. 2 and 54; Colonial Records of Connecticut, Vol. 1; Vol. 2, p. 91; Bavson's History of Gloucester, p. 51 to 67; Caulkin's History of New London, pp. 84, 85 and 158.

68. Albert Judson Fisher.

RICHARD CARDER.—Of Boston, Mass., Portsmouth and Warwick, R. I., May 25, 1636, was a freeman; March 7, 1638, he was one of 19 signers of the compact of Portsmouth; 1659-60-63, he was Commissioner. In 1664 to 1666 he was Deputy to General Court. In 1666 he was chosen Assistant, but refused.

REFERENCE: Austin's Genealogical Dictionary of Rhode Island.

39. George Samuel Marsh.

WILLIAM CARPENTER—Of Providence, R. I., was Deputy in 1664-5, 1675, 1676 and 1679; Assistant to the Governor, 1665 to 1672.

REFERENCE: Austin's Genealogical Dictionary, p. 37; Society of Colonial Wars Year Book, 1895, p. 207.

  39. George Samuel Marsh.

CAPTAIN JOHN CARTER.—[1616-1692]—Of Woburn, Mass.; Ensign, 1651; Lieutenant, 1664; Captain, 1672; Captain of Woburn Company in King Philip's War.

REFERENCE: Year Book of the Society of Colonial Wars.

  1. Seymour Morris.
  28. Cyrus Austin Hardy.

JOSIAH CHAPIN.—Was captain of Mass. Colonial forces at Mendon; Sergeant, 1685; Ensign, 1687; Lieutenant, 1689, and captain, 1692; was representative many years.

REFERENCE: Annals of Mendon (Metcalf) pp. 98, 104, 106, 108, 114, 126; Mass. Archives, Vol. 107, p. 161; Vol. 70, p. 296-97.

  10. Edward Milton Adams.
  49. Frank Eugene Spooner.
  51. Franklin Adams Meacham.

DEACON SAMUEL CHAPIN.—Springfield, Mass. For many years was appointed with John Pynchon and Eleazer Holyoke by the General Court of Mass. Bay Colony to administer the government of Springfield. At the burning of Springfield, Oct. 5, 1675, during King Philip's War, he was a participant in repelling the attacking Indians from the fortified houses.

REFERENCE: History of Springfield, p. 19 and 35, by Morris; Mass. Col. Records, Vol. 4, part 1, p. 115, 136, 213, 214, 379; History of Springfield by Mason A. Greene, p. 100, 124, 162, 578; Savage's Gen. Dictionary American Ancestry, Vol. 7; Chapin Family, p 239; Morris' Historic Address, "The Burning of Springfield," p. 35.

  68. Albert Judson Fisher.

SETH CHAPIN.—(Son of Josiah). Was captain of Mass. Colonial forces at Mendon, 1714, and later; was representative many years.

REFERENCE: Annals of Mendon (Metcalf), p. 169-208.

  10. Edward Milton Adams.
  49. Frank Eugene Spooner.
  51. Franklin Adams Meacham.

LIEUTENANT JOHN CHATFIELD.—Was commissioned ensign in Parish of Oxford, Conn., Oct., 1743; was commissioned Lieutenant of second company Derby, Oct., 1750.

REFERENCE: Connecticut Colonial Records; Vol. 8, p. 566; Vol. 9, p. 554.

 52. Hobart Chatfield Chatfield-Taylor.

CAPTAIN DANIEL CLARK.—[1622-1710]—Secretary of Colony, 1658-64, and 1665-6. Lieutenant of first body of cavalry in Connecticut, 1658; Captain of same troop in 1664; in 1666 appointed by the General Court with Governor Winthrop to call out the militia and commissioned officers in case of the invasion of the enemy of the colony, 1658-66.

REFERENCE: Ancient Windsor, Vol. 1, p. 125; Vol. 2, p. 153; Salisbury, Vol. 3, p. 230.

 21. William Wolcott Strong.
 42. Charles Thomson Atkinson.
 71. Ebenezer Lane.

JOHN CLARKE.—Was one of the corporation named in the charter of Connecticut granted by King Charles II. He was deputy to the General Court twenty-one sessions. Commissioner for Saybrook in 1664; was a soldier in the great battle of Pequot Indians of Mystic in 1637.

REFERENCE: Colonial Records of Connecticut, Vol. 1, p. 3, Vol. 2, p. 13; Society of Colonial Wars Year Book, 1895, p. 211.

 70. Charles Ridgely.

AARON CLEVELAND.—Of Woburn, Mass. Was in Capt. John Cutler's Co. which was engaged in Sudbury, Lancaster, Marlborough and vicinity during King Philip's War.

REFERENCE: N. E. Hist. and Gen. Reg., Vol. 42, p. 299.

 10. Edward Milton Adams.
 51. Franklin Adams Meacham.

CAPTAIN JOSIAH CLEVELAND.—[1713-1793]—Of Canterbury, Conn., May, 1759, was commissioned captain of the 9th Company or Train Band of the 11th Connecticut Regiment.

REFERENCE: Colonial Records of Connecticut, Vol. 11, p. 267.

 18. Scott Jordan.

JOSIAH CLEVELAND.—[1667-1709]—Of Woburn and Chelmsford, Mass., and Canterbury, Conn. Served as a private in the Indian War, 1688-9; also in the garrison in the West Regiment of Middlesex, 1691-2.

REFERENCE: Cleveland Genealogy; New England Historical and Genealogical Register, Vol. 43, p. 373; Savage's Genealogical Dictionary, Vol. 2, p. 406; Sewall's History of Woburn, Mass., p. 601; Society of Colonial Wars Year Book, 1895, p. 211.

 18. Scott Jordan.

MOSES CLEVELAND.—[1624-1701-2]—Of Woburn. Was a member of the militia company in 1676. Was also in garrison at Chelmsford, Mass., Nov. 20, 1675, and was a soldier in King Philip's War.

REFERENCE: New England Historical and Genealogical Register, Vol. 43, pp. 261 and 279.

10. Edward Milton Adams.
18. Scott Jordan.
51. Franklin Adams Meacham.

ROBERT COATES.—Of Lynn, Mass., was under Capt. Turner at Hadley, Mass., constituting one of the garrison at that place from April 6, 1676, to Aug. 24, 1676, and later.

REFERENCE: Mass. Archives, Vol. 68, p. 212; N. E. Hist. and Gen. Reg., Vol. 41, p. 29; Vol. 43, p. 264; Society of Colonial Wars Year Book, 1894, p. 95.

10. Edward Milton Adams.

CORPORAL EDWARD COBURN.—[1618 ——]—Was a soldier in the local military company at Chelmsford during King Philip's War, 1676, also during the French and Indian War, 1689. Was in command of Coburn's Garrison on the east side of the Merrimac River.

REFERENCE: Savage's Gen. Dict., Vol. 1, p. 423.

2. Captain Philip Reade.

DANIEL COLE.—Member of Yarmouth Military Company, 1643.

REFERENCE: Pierce's Colonial Lists, p. 74.

58. Frederick Laforrest Merrick.

WILLIAM COLLIER.—[—— 1670]—Was Governor's Assistant twenty-eight years, from 1634 to 1665, Plymouth Colony; was Commissioner to the United Colonies, 1643. Representative Plymouth Colony, was member of the Colonial "Council of War," Sept. 27, 1642 and later.

REFERENCE: Pierce's Colonial Lists, p. 4-85; Plymouth Colony Records, 1633-1670; Society of Colonial Wars Year Book, 1895; Savage's Gen. Dictionary, Vol. 1, p. 433.

10. Edward Milton Adams.
15. Josiah Lewis Lombard.
50. Albert Eugene Snow.
51. Franklin Adams Meacham.
61. Victor Clifton Alderson.
63. Rev. Abbott Eliot Kittredge.

GEORGE COLTON.—[—— 1699]—Of Longmeadow, Mass., Quartermaster.

REFERENCE: N. E. Hist. and Gen. Register, Vol. 33, p. 202.

42. Chas. Thomson Atkinson.

LOT CONANT, JR.—Of Beverly, Mass., was soldier in Capt. Joseph Gardiner's Company in King Philip's War, 1675-6, at the Great Swamp fight.

REFERENCE: Society of Colonial Wars Year Book, 1895, p. 212; Savage's Gen. Dictionary.

17. Frederick Clifton Pierce.

ROGER CONANT.—Was Governor of the Massachusetts Colony at Cape Ann, 1625-6, and at Salem, 1627-9. Deputy later.

REFERENCE: Society of Colonial Wars Year Book, 1895, p. 212; Savage's Gen. Dictionary.

17. Frederick Clifton Pierce.
60. John Conant Long.

LIEUTENANT JAMES CONVERSE.—[1620-1715]—Of Charlestown and Woburn, Mass. Lieutenant of Woburn Company in Garrison in King Philip's War; Deputy, 1679.

REFERENCE: Year Book, Society of Colonial Wars.

1. Seymour Morris.
28. Cyrus Austin Hardy.

MAJOR JAMES CONVERSE.—[1645-1705]—Of Woburn, Mass. Deputy to the General Court five times, 1679, 1680, 1683-1686, 1689, 1691, 1693; Speaker, 1699, 1702-3; Commander in defense of Storer's Garrison, 1691-1692, for which service he was made Major.

REFERENCE: Year Book, Society of Colonial Wars, p. 185-188; "Magnalia Christi Americana," by Rev. Cotton Mather, p. 613-18; Morris Genealogy, p. 38 to 50; Woburn Records of Births, Marriages and Deaths.

1. Seymour Morris.
28. Cyrus Austin Hardy.

CAPTAIN JOSIAH CONVERSE.—[1684]—Woburn, Leicester and Brookfield, Mass. Representative to the General Court, 1715. Captain of the Woburn Company.

REFERENCE: Year Book of the Society of Colonial Wars, 1894; Sewell's History of Woburn, Mass.; History of Leicester, Mass.

1. Seymour Morris.

LIEUTENANT JOSIAH CONVERSE.—[1710-1775]—Of Woburn and Leicester, Mass., and Stafford, Conn.; Representative to the General Court, 1733, from Leicester; Lieutenant of the Leicester Company.

REFERENCE: Year Book of Society of Colonial Wars, 1894; History of Leicester, Mass.

1. Seymour Morris.

MAJOR AARON COOK.—[1610-1690]—Westfield, Mass. Deputy to General Court, 1668; Ensign, 1676; Captain of Garrison in King Philip's War; Major of Hartford Troops, 1687.

REFERENCE: Ancient Windsor, Vol. 2, p. 160; Colonial Wars Year Book, 1895.

42. Charles Thomson Atkinson.
43. Harry Linn Wright.
45. Francis Porter Fisher.

CAPTAIN AARON COOK.—[1641-1716]—Ensign, 1663; Captain, 1678-1713, Hadley Militia. Deputy, 1689-91-93-97.

REFERENCE: Society of Colonial Wars Year Book, 1895, p. 213.

42. Charles Thomson Atkinson.
43. Harry Linn Wright.
45. Francis Porter Fisher.

MOSES COOK.—Killed in King Philip's War, Westfield, 1676.

REFERENCE: Savage's Genealogical Dictionary, N. E., p. 448; Ancient Windsor.

42. Charles Thomson Atkinson.

SAMUEL COOK.—Was commissioned Lieutenant at Wallingford, Conn., Oct., 1741. He was promoted Captain, Oct., 1742.

REFERENCE: Connecticut Colonial Records, Vol. 1735-1743, p. 418-488.

59. Charles Pratt Whitney.

THADDEUS COOK.—Was commissioned Ensign of Second Company of Preston, Conn., in Eighth Conn. Regiment in Oct., 1755. Lieutenant in Troop of Horse, Tenth Conn. Regiment in Oct., 1757; Captain of Second Company or train band at Preston, Conn., in May, 1763; Captain of troop of horse in Tenth Conn. Regiment in May, 1764. He was Deputy from Wallingford, Conn., to the General Court, 1775.

REFERENCE: Connecticut Colonial Records, Vol. 1751-1757, p. 414; Vol. 1757-1762, p. 69; Vol. 1762-1767, p. 142-255; Vol. 1775-1776, p. 2-91; Vol. 1776, p. 29.

59. Charles Pratt Whitney.

FRANCIS COOKE.—[1583-1663]—Came over in the Mayflower. Served in expedition against Indians, under Capt. Myles Standish, February 16, 1621. Member of the Plymouth Military Company, June 22, 1644.

REFERENCE: Society of Colonial Wars Year Book, 1895, p. 213.

34. Hempstead Washburne.
72. Lester Orestes Goddard.

LIEUTENANT THOMAS COOPER.—[1619-1675]—Of Springfield, Mass. Lieutenant of the Springfield Company. When the Indians attacked Brookfield, Mass., August 7, 1675, Lieut. Cooper commanded the rescuing force of twenty-seven dragoons and the Springfield Indians; was in command at Springfield, Mass., and was killed by the Indians at the burning of that town on Oct. 5, 1675; in 1668 was representative to the General Court of Massachusetts Bay Colony.

REFERENCE: Records of Society of Colonial Wars; Hubbard's "History of Western Massachusetts," and "History of New England;" "Massachusetts Bay Colonial Records;" History of Springfield, Mass.; History of North Brookfield, Mass.; History of Hadley, Mass.

68. Albert Judson Fisher.

WILLIAM CROMWELL.—A member of the Legislative Council of Lord Proprietor of Maryland, Lord Baltimore. He was paid forty pounds of tobacco by the Assembly of Maryland in November, 1678, for services rendered in an expedition against the Nanticoke Indians in the same year.

REFERENCE: Archives of Maryland Records, 1678-1683, p. 96; Genealogy of Chenoweth and Cromwell Families; History of Virginia, p. 341.

11. Charles Cromwell.

JAMES CUDWORTH.—[—— 1682]—Was representative, 1649-56-59; Assistant, 1656-8; Captain of Militia; commanded in early part of King Philip's War the whole force of Plymouth Colony; Deputy Governor in 1681.

REFERENCE: Savage's Genealogical Dictionary.

24. Lemuel Ruggles Hall.

JOHN CUNNABELL.—[1649-50 ——]—Was member of the company of Capt. William Turner, for services in King Philip's War. The company defended Northampton against the Indians, March 14, 1676, and defeated the Indians at the battle of "Great Falls," May 18, 1676. (For his services under Capt. Turner he received £3 8s 6d, as per journal of John Hull, who was treasurer of Massachusetts Colony, 1675-1680.)

REFERENCE: New England Historical and Gen. Register; Newcomb Genealogy; Cunnabell Genealogy.

38. George Whitfield Newcomb.

ENSIGN JAMES CUTLER.—[1606-1694]—Soldier in King Philip's War.

REFERENCE. Year Book 1894, Society of Colonial Wars; New England Genealogical and Historical Register, Vol. 37, p. 74.

25. Frank Baker.

LIEUTENANT THOMAS CUTLER.—[1648-1722]—Lieutenant of the Lexington Company.

REFERENCE: Hudson's History of Lexington, p. 49.

25. Frank Baker.

RICHARD CUTT.—Came from England prior to 1646; died 1676; was made Captain in command of fort built at Great Island, 1660; represented Portsmouth several times in the General Court between 1655 and 1676.

REFERENCE: Adam's Portsmouth, p. 48; History of Cutt family.

46. George Butters.

LIEUTENANT ELIHU DAGGETT.—Oct. 16, 1754, Lieutenant in Capt. John Stearnes' Company; April 6, 1757, private in Capt. John Stearnes' Company, alarm soldiers.

REFERENCE: French and Indian War Rolls; Vol. 93, p. 142; Vol. 95, p. 261.

66. Daniel Charles Daggett.

SAMUEL DAMON.—A soldier in the Narragansett or King Philip's War from Reading, Mass.

REFERENCE: Mass. Archives, Vol. 68, p. 79-100.

39. George Samuel Marsh.

MAJOR GENERAL DANIEL DENISON.—Massachusetts Colonial forces, who was appointed Captain (during the Pequot War), 1637, and Major General from 1652 to 1680. Deputy to the General Court, 1635-52. Colonial Secretary, 1653. Commissioner for the United Colonies, 1654-62.

REFERENCE: Society of Colonial Wars Year Book, 1895, p. 216; Savage's Gen. Dict.

54. William Ward Wight.

CAPTAIN GEORGE DENISON.—Captain of Roxbury, Mass., train band, 1646; campaigned against Narragansetts, 1654, also 1675; was at "Swamp Fight." In 1676 was appointed by Connecticut Council second in command of all Connecticut forces; was deputy to Legislature fifteen different times, 1671-1694.

REFERENCE: Society of Colonial Wars Year Book, 1894, p. 30-83; Connecticut Colonial Records, 1662-94.

10. Edward Milton Adams.
51. Franklin Adams Meacham.

GEORGE DENISON, JR.—Was appointed Commissary of Connecticut forces in New London County, 1703.

REFERENCE: Connecticut Colonial Records, Vol. 1689-1706, p. 458.

10. Edward Milton Adams.
51. Franklin Adams Meacham.

JOHN DENISON.—Of Stonington, Conn., was Ensign in Colonial forces, Aug. 7, 1673 and later; Was Deputy many years.

REFERENCE: Connecticut Colonial Records, 1665, p. 206.

10. Edward Milton Adams.
51. Franklin Adams Meacham.

DANIEL DENNY.—Captain of Militia at Leicester, Mass.; representative to the General Court, 1745-46-47.

REFERENCE: History of Leicester, Mass., 1860; Denny Genealogy, 1886.

5. John Smith Sargent.

JOHN DOANE.—[1591-1686]—Of Plymouth and Eastham; Governor's Assistant, 1632-3; Governor's Assistant, 1639, "to make laws for the Colony;" member of Plymouth Military Company, 1643; Deputy from Plymouth, 1639-42; from Eastham, 1649-50-53-59.

REFERENCE: Plymouth Colony Records, Vol. 1, p. 5-121; Pierce's Colonial Lists, p. 76.

18. Scott Jordan.

COMMISSARY WILLIAM DOUGLAS.—[1610-1682]—Gloucester and Boston, Mass., and New London, Conn. Commissioner of New London, 1667; Representative to the General Court, 1672, and thereafter; Commissary to the army during King Philip's War.

REFERENCE: Savage's Gen. Dict. of N. E.; Connecticut Colonial Records, Vol. 4, p. 289; Vol. 2, p. 442-455; Vol. 6, p. 489; Vol. 7, p. 468; Caulkin's History of New London.

68. Albert Judson Fisher.

LIEUTENANT JOHN DRESSER.—[1639-1724]—Member of the Provincial forces of Massachusetts Bay. Deputy, 1691, and for several years thereafter from Rowley, Mass.

REFERENCE: Society of Colonial Wars Year Book, 1895, p. 218.

6. Lyman Dresser Hammond.

CAPTAIN RICHARD DRESSER.—[1714-1797]—Captain of the Charlton, Mass., Company in Col. John Chandler's Regiment, that marched to the relief of Ft. William Henry, Aug. 10, 1758, French and Indian War.

REFERENCE: Massachusetts Archives, Vol. 95, p. 519.

6. Lyman Dresser Hammond.

ABRAHAM DU BOIS.—Served in the second Canadian expedition against the French.

REFERENCE: New York Colonial Manuscripts, English, Vol. 60, p. 188.

13. Samuel Eberly Gross.

LOUIS DUBOIS.—French Huguenot settler and patentee of large land tract in eastern New York. Founder of the Huguenot settlement, New Paltz, in Ulster County. His wife, Catherine (Blanshan) DuBois, and her three children, with others, were carried into captivity by the Indians at the burning of Hurley (New Village), June 7, 1663. Louis DuBois led an expedition against the Indians, which defeated them in battle and effected the rescue of the captives. In 1670 he served again in the Colonial forces against the Indians, who were then on the war path. Was Magistrate in 1673, and after, at New Village and Marbleton; also was founder and First Elder of the French Reform Church of New Paltz.

REFERENCE: "American Ancestry," Vol. 1, p. 24-25; J. B. Beers' "History of Green County, New York;" Brodhead's "History of New York," Vol. 1, p. 657-678-711-714; Ibid., Vol. 2, p. 311-312; N. Y. Historic Documents, Vol. 13, p. 338-350; N. Y Col. Archives, Vol. 13, p. 450; N. Y. Col. Archives, Vol. 13, p. 448; Schoonmaker's His. of Kingston, N. Y., p. 41-60-71-72-243-478.

13. Samuel Eberly Gross.

LIEUTENANT SOLOMON DUBOIS.—Lieutenant of the Ulster County Militia during early Colonial wars, given in list of the "Commanding Officers as well Milletery and Sivel," in 1728; in an Ulster County roster of "Old Ofesers and Old Men," as the name was spelled at that time: Lieut Sallomon DuBoys.

REFERENCE: Documentary History of the State of New York, Vol. 2, p. 588.

13. Samuel Eberly Gross.

FRANCIS DUDLEY.—A soldier in King Philip's War.

REFERENCE: Society of Colonial Wars Year Book, 1894, p. 53; Spooner Genealogy; Dudley Genealogy; Putnam's Monthly Historical Magazine.

    49. Frank Eugene Spooner.

GOVERNOR THOMAS DUDLEY.—Came to America in 1630; was Governor or Deputy Governor of Massachusetts Bay Colony from 1634 to 1640, being third Governor of the Colony. Assistant, 1635-36-41-44. Continuously in office 22 years. Commissioner for the United Colonies, 1643-47-49. Twice President of the United Colonies, Major General or commander of all the military forces in the Colony in 1644 and was again Governor from 1645 to 1650.

REFERENCE: Society of Colonial Wars Year Book, 1895, p. 60 and 219; Massachusetts Colonial Records, 1630-1653; Appleton's Cyclopedia of American Biography, p. 243; Savage's Genealogical Dictionary; Ruggles Genealogy, p. 141-2-3; Humphrey Genealogy; Dudley Genealogy; Woodbridge Genealogy; New England Historical and Genealogical Register; Suffield, Conn., Simsbury, Conn., Norfolk, Conn., town and church records; Southfield, Mass., church records.

    4. William Ruggles Tucker.
    5. John Smith Sargent.
    10. Edward Milton Adams.
    19. Jonathan Edwards Woodbridge.
    24. Lemuel Ruggles Hall.
    54. William Ward Wight.

JOHN DUMBLETON, JR.—[1658-1675]—Killed by Indians during King Philip's War at Westfield, Mass., Oct. 27, 1675.

REFERENCE: Savage's Gen. Dict.; History of Hadley, p. 156, by Judd; Holland's "History of Western Mass.," p. 106-107; Sprague's Historic Address, p. 24; Markham's "History of King Philip's War," p. 123-155; Hubbard's "Indian Wars in New England," p. 127.

    68. Albert Judson Fisher.

WILLIAM EAGER.—(Ager, Agur) was private in Capt. Thomas Prentiss' Company of "Middlesex" troopers in Mt. Hope campaign; his name appears on roll of Aug. 27, 1675; he was also in same company under Lieut. Edward Oakes, 1675-6.

REFERENCE: N. E. Hist. and Gen. Reg., Vol. 47, p. 280-4.

    52. Hobart Chatfield Chatfield-Taylor.

SAMUEL EDDY.—Of Plymouth, Mass.; member of the Plymouth Military Company in August, 1643.

REFERENCE: Pierce's Colonial Lists, p. 76.

    67. John Demmon Vandercook.

ROBERT ELLIOTT.—Representative to General Court; President of Council of Province of N. H.
 REFERENCE: Provincial Records, N. H.; Savage's Dictionary.
 46. George Butters.

EDWARD ELMER, SR.—A soldier in King Philip's War, and killed in June, 1676.
 REFERENCE: S. C. W. 1895 Year Book.
 39. George Samuel Marsh.

SERGEANT JOHN EMERY, JR.—[1629-1693]—Of Newbury, Mass.; soldier under Major Samuel Appleton, Dec. 19, 1675, at the "Great Swamp Fight." Served in Capt. Samuel Brocklebank's Company.
 REFERENCE: Soldiers of King Philip's War, 1675-7, p. 109-159-310; Coffin's History of Newbury, p. 145; N. E. Hist. and Gen. Register, Vol. 27, p. 423.
 2. Captain Philip Reade.

CAPTAIN JOHN EVERETT.—[1636-1714]—Dedham, Mass. In 1695 commanded a company of fifty or sixty Massachusetts soldiers, raised and sent by the Massachusetts Colony to assist the New Hampshire Colony against the Indians. Stationed at Exeter and Portsmouth, N. H., and after eleven months ordered into Maine.
 REFERENCE: Savage's Genealogical Dictionary; N. H. Provincial Papers, Vol. 11, p. 153-157-158-169; "Acts and Resolves of the Province of Mass. Bay," Vol. 7; Resolves, 1692-1702, Appendix 2, p. 521.
 68. Albert Judson Fisher.

LIEUTENANT DAVID FARNSWORTH.—[1711 ——]—Of Charlestown and Hollis, N. H. On April 20, 1757, he was taken prisoner by party of seventy French and Indians and carried to Canada. Some years later he was redeemed and returned home.
 REFERENCE: Farnsworth Genealogy, p. 87; Saunderson's History of Charlestown, p. 14-335.
 4. William Ruggles Tucker.

SAMUEL FARNSWORTH.—[1669 ——]—A member of the Garrison of Groton, Mass., March 17, 1691-2.
 REFERENCE: N. E. Hist. and Gen. Register for 1889, p. 374.
 4. William Ruggles Tucker.

STEPHEN FARNSWORTH.—Was captured by the Indians, April 19, 1746, and taken to Montreal, where he was confined. He was also one of Capt. Stevens' company, raised for the defense of "No. 4;" company formed June 21, 1750.

REFERENCE: History of Charlestown, N. H., p. 342.

67. John Demmon Vandercook.

JACOB FARRAR.—One of the seven victims killed and mutilated by the Indians in Monaco's raid upon Lancaster, Aug. 27, 1675, during King Philip's War.

REFERENCE: Nourse's "Military Annals of Lancaster," p. 10; Savage's Genealogical Dictionary; Year Book Society of Colonial Wars, 1895; Marvin's History of Lancaster, p. 59-102.

68. Albert Judson Fisher.

ANTHONY FISHER, JR.—[—— 1670]—Dedham, Mass., in 1637; member of Ancient and Honorable Artillery Company in 1644.

REFERENCE: Savage's Genealogical Dictionary; Whitman's History of A. and H. Artillery Company, p. 143; Mass. Bay Colonial Records, Vol. 4, part 1, p. 117.

68. Albert Judson Fisher.

LIEUTENANT JOHN FLINT.—Lieutenant in Capt. Thomas Hinchman's troop, composed of troopers in Sudbury, Marlborough, Concord, Mass. Was a deputy from Concord, Mass., to serve at the General Court.

REFERENCE: Official Records of the General Court of Massachusetts, Vol. 5, p. 132-210-260-350-1; Genealogical Register of the Descendants of Thomas Flint of Salem; History of Antrim, p. 495.

56. Wyman Kneeland Flint.

SERGEANT THOMAS FLINT.—Of Salem Village, Danvers, Mass., in 1638, and of Redding, after 1644. Was in Capt. Joseph Gardiner's troop, Dec. 10-16, 1675; also in Capt. Curwin's troop and in the troop commanded by Capt. Thomas Prentice. Was in the Reserve Salem Old Troop.

REFERENCE: Mass. Archives, Vol. 68, p. 73-93-104-119, also Vol. 69, p. 217; Bodge, p. 41-117-118; Gen. History of Reading, Mass., by Lilley Eaton, 1874; Gen. Reg. Descendants of Thos. Flint of Salem, p. 10-11, by John Flint, and J. H. Stone.

2. Capt. Philip Reade.

GERRIT FOKAR.—Served in Capt. Pawling's foot company of Hurley soldiers, doing duty at Marbleton, N. Y., during Esopus Indian Wars.

REFERENCE: New York Colonial Manuscripts, Vol. 22, p. 99 and following; New York Historical Documents, Vol. 13, p. 246 and following.

    13. Samuel Eberly Gross.

EDMUND FREEMAN.—[1589-1682]—Of Sandwich, Mass.; member of Colonial "War" Council, Sept. 27, 1642; Assistant Plymouth Colony, 1640-45; member of council of war to provide troops for the safety of the Colony against the Indians, 1642, Plymouth Colony.

REFERENCE: Pierce's Colonial Lists, p. 4-85, also Plymouth Colonial Records, Vol. 1, p. 140.

    50. Albert Eugene Snow.
    58. Frederick Laforrest Merrick.
    61. Victor Clifton Alderson.

JOHN FREEMAN.—Was a member of Military Company, Sandwich, Mass., 1643; commissioned Ensign at Eastham, March, 1655; Lieutenant of Cavalry Company; commissioned Oct. 2, 1659; Assistant of Plymouth Colony, 1667, 1678 and 1682-86; was Lieutenant and second in command under Major Josiah Winslow, who, with 102 men, marched against Awashouk, the Squaw, Sachem, of Saconett, near Assonet, July 8, 1671; was member of Eastham town "War" Council, Feb. 29, 1675; was appointed Major of 3d Plymouth Colony Regiment, composed of companies from Barnstable, Eastham, Sandwich and Yarmouth.

REFERENCE: Pierce's Colonial Lists, p. 68-73-94-97-98; Plymouth Colonial Records, Vol. 3, p. 74-174; Vol. 4, p. 147; N. E. H. and G. Register, Vol. 20, p. 59-60.

    50. Albert Eugene Snow.
    58. Frederick Laforrest Merrick.
    61. Victor Clifton Alderson.

JACOB FRENCH.—[1640-1713]—Of Billerica; Sergeant of the Militia. His house used as a garrison house in 1676.

REFERENCE: N. E. Hist. and Gen. Register, Vol. 44, p. 368.

    73. Anthony French Merrill.

CORPORAL JOHN FRENCH.—Was wounded by the Indians in the assault at Quaboag in 1675.

REFERENCE: Society of Colonial Wars Year Book, 1895, p. 224.

    63. Rev. Abbott Eliot Kittredge.

LIEUTENANT WILLIAM FRENCH.—[1603-1681]—Of Cambridge and Billerica, Mass.; Representative to the General Court, 1663; Lieutenant in King Philip's War, and afterwards Captain.

REFERENCE: Society of Colonial Wars Year Book, 1894, p. 184; Savage's Gen. Dict.; Hazen's His. of Billerica, Mass.; also general appendix to the same.

1. Seymour Morris.
52. Hobart Chatfield Chatfield-Taylor.
63. Rev. Abbott Eliot Kittredge.
73. Anthony French Merrill.

WILLIAM FRENCH—[1701-1775]—He was Lieutenant and served in war against the Indians, being on the muster roll of 1722.

REFERENCE: N. E. Hist. and Gen. Register, Vol. 44, p. 371.

73. Anthony French Merrill.

THOMAS FULLER.—Was Sergeant in 1656. Lieutenant in 1685 in Woburn and Wenham, Mass.

REFERENCE: Sewall's History of Woburn, p. 614; Massachusetts Colonial Records, Vol. 5, p. 56.

17. Frederick Clifton Pierce.

JOHN GERRISH.—[1646-1714]—Chosen Representative to General Court, 1684; member of convention, 1689; also Captain and Sheriff.

REFERENCE: Savage's Dictionary, N. E. H. and G., Vol. 6, p. 258.

46. George Butters.

COLONEL TIMOTHY GERRISH.—[1684-1756]—Dover, N. H. Captain of the Provincial Militia at Dover, 1719. Deputy, 1709-15-22. Colonel of the Provincial Militia of York County, Me., 1725. Royal Councillor of Province of Massachusetts, 1730-1735.

REFERENCE: Society of Colonial Wars Year Book, 1895, p. 226.

46. George Butters.

COLONEL JAMES GIBSON.—A retired British army officer, equipped at his own expense a company of 300 men and led them at the siege of Louisburg, Cape Breton in 1745.

REFERENCE: Windsor Memorial History of Breton, Vol. 2, p. 113-117; Parkman, Half Century of Conflict, Vol. 2, p. 86-100; Drake, "The Taking of Louisburg," p. 70; Year Book, Society of Colonial Wars, 1894, p. 209.

32. Rev. James Gibson Johnson.

JOHN GILBERT.—[—— 1654]—Of Dorchester and Taunton, Mass. In 1643 a member of the Military Company of Yarmouth, Mass., commanded by Lieut. Wm. Palmer.

REFERENCE: Pierce's Colonial Lists, p. 75.

4. William Ruggles Tucker.

JONATHAN GILBERT.—Rendered important services in the Indian wars. He was sent to one of the rebellious chiefs, Sequasson, by the Commissioners to summon him to their presence. He and John Griffin were sent as messengers to Chief Chickwallop and Manasanes by the Commissioners, but the Sagamores and Indians at Waranoke carried it insolently, etc. Sent by the Commissioners as a messenger to the chief of the Narragansetts during hostilities in 1652. Was sent by the Commissioners to chiefs of the Podunk Indians during hostilities in 1657.

REFERENCE: N. E. Reg., Vol. 4, p. 229-230-231-232.

36. Henry Lathrop Turner.

CAPTAIN EDWARD GODDARD.—[1675-1754]—Captain of troop; Deputy to General Court from Framingham, Mass., 1724-1731; three years in his Majesty's Council, 1733-36.

REFERENCE: Town records of Framingham, Mass.

31. Charles Newton Fessenden.

RICHARD GOODMAN.—Was elected inspector of arms at Hadley, Mass., on Dec. 16, 1664; was appointed by the County Court Sergeant of the Hadley Military Company in 1663; was killed by the Indians at Hockanum (near Northampton), Mass., on April 1, 1676, King Philip's War.

REFERENCE: Judd's History of Hadley, Mass., p. 165-226.

52. Hobart Chatfield Chatfield-Taylor.

CAPTAIN PHILIP GOODRIDGE.—Captain of Company in French and Indian War, 1755.

REFERENCE: Massachusetts Archives.

31. Charles Newton Fessenden.

CAPTAIN JOHN GORHAM.—Commanded second Plymouth Colony Company in Great Swamp Fight, 1675.

REFERENCE: Plymouth Colony Records, 1650-1676; S. C. W. 1894 Year Book.

10. Edward Milton Adams.
51. Franklin Adams Meacham.

SAMUEL GORTON.—Of Warwick, R. I. In 1649 Assistant; 1651-56-63, Commissioner; 1664-66-70, Deputy.
REFERENCE: Austin's Genealogical Dictionary of Rhode Island, p. 304.
39. George Samuel Marsh.

BENJAMIN GRAVES.—[1645 ——]—Of Concord, Mass.; soldier in Capt. Wheeler's Company in the Great Swamp Fight, 1675.
REFERENCE: N. E. Hist. and Gen. Register, Vol. 38, p. 40.
1. Seymour Morris.

JOHN GREEN.—Was a member of Lieut. Edward Oakes' troop in the winter of 1675-76. He was also Corporal under Lieut. William Hasey, August to October, 1675, King Philip's War.
REFERENCE: New England Historical and Genealogical Register, Vol. 37, p. 284; Vol. 42, p. 94.
17. Frederick Clifton Pierce.

THOMAS GRIDLEY.—Was soldier from Connecticut in the Pequot War, 1637.
REFERENCE: Society of Colonial Wars Year Book, 1895, p. 230.
33. Deming Haven Preston.

JOHN GRIFFIN.—Of Windsor. Deputy, 1670. Appointed by the Legislature temporary commander of the Simsbury Train Band, 1673, confirmed Sergeant and Chief in command, 1675.
REFERENCE: Mass. and Conn. Colonial Records; Stiles' History of Windsor; Humphrey Genealogy.
10. Edward Milton Adams.
33. Deming Haven Preston.

EDWARD GRISWOLD.—Built "Old Fort" Springfield; Deputy to General Court from Windsor and Killingworth for many years.
REFERENCE: Ancient Windsor ——, Vol. 7, p. 350-351.
42. Charles Thomson Atkinson.

GOVERNOR MATTHEW GRISWOLD.—[1714-1789]—In 1739 Captain of the South Train Band of Lyme, Conn.; 1766, Major of Third Regiment of Horse and Foot; 1751, Representative; 1759-1765, member of Governor's Council; 1766-69, Chief Justice; 1771-84, Deputy Governor and Lieutenant Governor of Connecticut; 1784-86, Governor.
REFERENCE: Magazine of American History, Vol. 11, p. 218-237.
71. Ebenezer Lane.

LIEUTENANT MATTHEW GRISWOLD.—[1620-1698]—Of Windsor and Lyme, Conn. Lieutenant of the Lyme Train Band. Deputy, 1654-1667, 1668, 1678, 1685.

REFERENCE: Connecticut Colonial Records, 1678-1689, p. 3-27-181; Magazine of American History, Vol. 11, p. 131.

71. Ebenezer Lane.

JAMES HADLOCK.—Served in Capt. John Holbrook's company in King Philip's War, Aug. 24, 1676.

REFERENCE: N. E. Hist. and Gen. Register, Vol. 42, p. 99.

6. Lyman Dresser Hammond.

CAPTAIN WALTER HAINES.—[1583-1655]—Of Watertown, Mass., 1638; Sudbury, 1639; built the Haines Garrison on the west side, which sustained the burden of the fight in the memorable Indian attack upon Sudbury during King Philip's War, April 21, 1675; member of the Ancient and Honorable Artillery Company in 1639; Representative for Sudbury from 1641 to 1651.

REFERENCE: Hudson's "Annals of Sudbury, Wayland and Maynard," p. 4-8-10-13-14-15; Whitman's "History Ancient" Honorable Artillery Co., Ed. 1842, p. 97; N. E. Hist. and Gen. Register, Vol. 47, p. 72; Vol. 39, p. 263-264; Vol. 2, p. 108, Savage's Genealogical Dictionary; "Porter Family History," Vol. 1, p. 26.

68. Albert Judson Fisher.

CAPTAIN EZEKIEL HALE.—[1725-1789]—Of Newbury and Dracut, Mass. Served in the French War, 1758-61. In 1755 or 1756 went to Albany in Colonel Ephraim Williams' Regiment, in command of Sir William Johnson (Seven Years' War). He was a Lieutenant in the 6th Foot Company of Newbury in 1761.

REFERENCE: Genealogy of the Hale family, p. 180; New England Historical and Genealogical Register, Vol. 21, p. 83-98.

2. Captain Philip Reade.

SERGEANT THOMAS HALE.—[1633-1688]—Of Newbury, Mass., having been authorized "to carry on the military exercise there," was appointed, etc., 1652-57.

REFERENCE: Records of the Colony of Mass. Bay, Vol. 3, p. 290; Vol. 4, p. 117; N. E. Historical and Genealogical Register, Vol. 31; Hale Genealogy.

2. Captain Philip Reade.

CAPTAIN THOMAS HALE.—[1658-9-1730]—Of Newbury and Rowley, Mass., was Captain in the Militia.

REFERENCE: Genealogy of the descendants of Thomas Hale of Newbury, Massachusetts Archives, 114-178-450-501.

2. Captain Philip Reade.

ANDREW HALLETT, SR.—Was in Lieut. William Palmer's Company at Yarmouth, Mass., Aug., 1643.

REFERENCE: Pierce's Colonial Lists, p. 74.

4. William Ruggles Tucker.
37. Frank Bassett Tobey.

SERGEANT EBENEZER HAMMOND.—[1714]—Of Charlton, Mass. Sergeant of a detachment of Capt. Jonathan Tooker's Company in Col. John Chandler's Regiment in the French and Indian War, marching to the relief of Ft. William Henry, under command of Joshua Meriam as their captain. Lieutenant of the First Regiment of Militia in County of Worcester, Mass., March 1, 1763, in Capt. Paul Wheelock's Company of Charlton.

REFERENCE: Massachusetts Archives, Vol. 95, p. 517; Vol. 99, p. 519.

6. Lyman Dresser Hammond.

SAMUEL HARLOW.—[1652 ——]—Sergeant in Commander James Warren's Plymouth South Company on Roll, 1699.

REFERENCE: History of Plymouth Co.; Davis Landmarks of Plymouth, p. 128.

46. George Butters.

CAPTAIN THOMAS HART.—Of Farmington, Conn. Ensign, 1678; Lieutenant, 1693; Captain, 1695; Deputy, 1690-1711; Speaker, 1700-06.

REFERENCE: Society of Colonial Wars Year Book, 1895, p. 232.

33. Deming Haven Preston.

JOHN HASTINGS.—[1653 ——]—Of Watertown, Mass. A member of Capt. Davenport's Company in King Philip's War.

REFERENCE. N. E. Hist. and Gen. Register, Vol. 39, p. 259.

4. William Ruggles Tucker.
67. John Demmon Vandercook.

ANTHONY HAWKINS.—One of the patentees of Connecticut under charter from Charles II., April 29, 1662; Assistant, 1668-70; Deputy.

REFERENCE: Savage's Genealogical Dictionary, p. 382; Colonial Wars Year Book, 1895.

42. Charles Thomson Atkinson.

WILLIAM HATHORNE.—Of Salem, Mass. First Speaker of the House of Deputies, 1644; Assistant, 1662-79; Commissioner for the United Colonies in 1643; Captain of the Salem Company of Militia and Major of the Massachusetts Bay Colony, 1656.

REFERENCE: Society of Colonial Wars Year Book, 1895, p. 233.

30. Charles Durkee Dana.

JOHN HAYNES.—[1621-1692]—(Deacon). Was owner and Commander of a garrison house (block house) at Sudbury, Mass. Bay Colony. He served in Sir Wm. Phipps' Canadian expedition in 1690. Representative of Sudbury to General Court, 1668.

REFERENCE: Massachusetts Archives, Vol. 30, p. 205; New England Historical and Genealogical Register, Vol. 40, p. 398-399-400-403; Bodge's papers on King Philip's War; Hudson's Annals of Sudbury, p. 14-15-33, etc.; N. E. Hist. and Gen. Register, Vol. 47, p. 72; Savage's Gen. Dict. of N. E.

62. William Dorrance Messinger.
68. Albert Judson Fisher.

CAPTAIN SAMUEL HICKOX.—[1695-1765]—Of Waterbury. Captain of the Militia.

REFERENCE: History of Waterbury, Conn.

1. Seymour Morris.

SERGEANT SAMUEL HICKOX.—One of the original proprietors and grantee in the first Indian deed of Waterbury, Conn. Sergeant in the local militia.

REFERENCE:—History of Waterbury, Conn.

1. Seymour Morris.

CAPTAIN WILLIAM HICKOX.—[1673]—Of Waterbury, Conn.; an original proprietor; Captain of the Militia in 1727; Deputy to the General Court in 1728.

REFERENCE: History of Waterbury, Conn.

1. Seymour Morris.

ZACHARIAH HICKS.—Was private in Capt. Joseph Sill's Company of Massachusetts Bay troops, Aug. 24, 1676.

REFERENCE: New England Historical and Genealogical Register, Vol. 41, p. 409.

17. Frederick Clifton Pierce.

EPHRAIM HILDRETH.—Of Dracut. Served 21 weeks in Capt. Eleazer Tyng's Company in 1725.

REFERENCE: Massachusetts Archives, Vol. 61, p. 196.

2. Captain Philip Reade.

LIEUTENANT JAMES HILDRETH.—[1631-1695]—Of Chelmsford, Mass. Was Lieutenant in the Military Company.

REFERENCE: Middlesex Probate Records; Cambridge Probate Records, 1695.

2. Captain Philip Reade.

SERGEANT RICHARD HILDRETH.—[1605-1688]—Of Woburn. Prior to March 3, 1663, he was Sergeant in the Military Company at Chelmsford and served as such until 1664.

REFERENCE: Vol. 4, part 2, p. 100, Oct. 12, 1669, Gen. Court of the Colony of Mass. Bay in New England; History of Chelmsford.

2. Captain Philip Reade.

SAMUEL HINCKLEY.—Was a member of Lieut. Thomas Dimmock's (Dymock's) Company at Barnstable, Mass., Aug., 1643.

REFERENCE: Pierce's Colonial Lists, p. 73.

37. Frank Bassett Tobey.

GOVERNOR THOMAS HINCKLEY.—Deputy to Plymouth General Court, 1646; Assistant, 1658 to 1680; Commissioner of Plymouth Colony against King Philip, 1675-76; at Great Swamp Fight. Deputy Governor, 1680; Governor, 1681; Assistant of Province Massachusetts Bay.

REFERENCE: Society Colonial Wars Year Book, 1895, p. 235.

50. Albert Eugene Snow.

ANDREW HINMAN, SR.—Was commissioned Captain of South Company at Woodbury, Conn., on May 10, 1733.

REFERENCE: Hinman's Early Puritan Settlers; Connecticut Colonial Records, 1726-35, p. 431.

52. Hobart Chatfield Chatfield-Taylor.

TITUS HINMAN.—Was commissioned Lieutenant at Woodbury, Conn., on May 11, 1710; was promoted Captain May 13, 1714.

REFERENCE: Hinman's Early Puritan Settlers; **Connecticut Colonial Records**, 1706-16, p. 143-426.

52. Hobart Chatfield Chatfield-Taylor.

CAPTAIN LUKE HITCHCOCK, JR.—[1655-1727]—Soldier in King Philip's War. He served under Captain Turner in the Falls fight, May, 1676.

REFERENCE: N. E. Hist. and Gen. Register, Vol. 40, p. 212; Bates' Address in Westfield Centennial, p. 66; Hitchcock Family, p. 407-408-410; West Springfield Centennial; Mason A. Greene's History of Springfield, p. 166-193; Holland's History of Western Massachusetts, Vol. 2, p. 318; Chapin family, p. 292.

68. Albert Judson Fisher.

CAPTAIN LUKE HITCHCOCK, SR.—[—— 1659]—Of Wethersfield, Conn., 1644; soldier and Captain in early Colonial wars.

REFERENCE: Savage's Genealogical Dictionary; **American Ancestry**; History of Hitchcock Family, p. 205-206.

68. Albert Judson Fisher.

RANDALL HOLDEN.—Was Marshal and Corporal at Portsmouth, R. I., 1638; was member of Town Council of Warwick, R. I., 1647; was Assistant of the Colony, 1647-53 to 1658-64-5-76; Deputy to General Court of R. I. ten years during the period 1666-86; was Judge of the Court of Common Pleas, 1687-8; was called Captain in Col. Records, Oct 26, 1664.

REFERENCE: Austin's Genealogical Dictionary of R. I.; Savage's Genealogical Dictionary, Vol. 2, p. 445; R. I. Colonial Records, Vol 2 (1664-77), p. 22-37-61-72-91-150-30.

75. Warren Lippitt Beckwith.

LIEUTENANT JOHN HOLLISTER.—[1612-1665]—Of Wethersfield, Conn.; a Deputy to the General Court, 1644, and many times thereafter, till 1656; member of the Wethersfield Train Band.

REFERENCE: Society of Colonial Wars Year Book, 1894, p. 55.

1. Seymour Morris.

CAPTAIN STEPHEN HOLLISTER.—[1658-1709]—Of Wethersfield, Conn.; member of the Wethersfield Train Band.

REFERENCE: History of Waterbury, **Conn.**

1. Seymour Morris.

JOSHUA HOLMES.—Was Ensign in Connecticut Colonial forces at Stonington, Conn. He was appointed Oct., 1729.

REFERENCE: Connecticut Colonial Records, Vol. 1726-1735, p. 262.

  10. Edward Milton Adams.
  51. Franklin Adams Meacham.

GILES HOPKINS.—Volunteered for campaign against Pequot Indians, June 7, 1637.

REFERENCE: Plymouth Colony Records; Pierce's Colonial Lists, p. 84.

  58. Frederick Laforrest Merrick.
  63. Rev. Abbott Eliot Kittredge.

LIEUTENANT JOHN HOPKINS.—[1660-1732]—Of Waterbury, Conn.; Sergeant, 1714; Ensign, 1715; Lieutenant, 1716.

REFERENCE: History of Waterbury, Conn., p. 152.

  1. Seymour Morris.

STEPHEN HOPKINS.—Came in the Mayflower, 1620, a member of Capt. Myles Standish's Military Company, which was formed February, 1621. In summer of 1621 sent by Gov. Bradford with Edw. Winslow (afterward Governor) on a historic mission to King Massasoit. In 1633-36, a member of the Governor's Council; 1637, volunteered to go with other members of Colony to aid Massachusetts Bay and Connecticut Colonies in their war with the Pequots. In 1642, chosen one of a Council of War for Plymouth.

REFERENCE: Davis' Ancient Landmarks of Plymouth; New England Historical and Genealogical Register, Vol. 47, p. 81-83-186-187; Vol. 22, p. 60-63-191; Morton's memoranda, p. 68-74; Society of Colonial Wars Year Book, 1895, p. 236.

  15. Josiah Lewis Lombard.
  18. Scott Jordan.
  50. Albert Eugene Snow.
  58. Frederick Laforrest Merrick.
  63. Rev. Abbott Eliot Kittredge.

WILLIAM HOPKINS.—Assistant Governor, 1641-2.

REFERENCE: Savage's Genealogical Dictionary.

  42. Charles Thomson Atkinson.

SERGEANT WILLIAM HOUGH.—Of Gloucester, Mass., and New London, Conn. Was Sergeant of the first Military Company of New London. Member of committee on fortifications.

REFERENCE: Savage's Genealogical Dictionary of N. E.; Caulkin's History of New London, Conn., p. 183-300; Babson's History of Gloucester, Mass., p. 105; Connecticut Colonial Records, Vol. 3, p. 241.

  68. Albert Judson Fisher.

JOHN HOUGHTON, JR.—[1650-1737]—Town Clerk of Lancaster from 1686 to 1725; soldier in garrison of Lawrence Waters at Lancaster in King Philip's War, 1676, and in garrison of Capt. Thos. Wilder in 1704. He had a garrison house in 1711. Was Magistrate; Representative to the General Court fourteen years, between 1693 and 1724.

REFERENCE: Nourse's "Early Records of Lancaster," p. 173-339; Willard's "Centennial Address," p. 95; Marvin's "History of Lancaster," p. 110-144-668-669-739-740; Mass. Archives, Vol. 71, p. 876; "American Ancestry," Vol. 9, p. 113.

68. Albert Judson Fisher.

JOHN HOUGHTON, SR.—At Lancaster, Mass., 1653-1684. During King Philip's War, after second Indian attack upon Lancaster, Feb. 10, 1676, he served in the Lawrence Waters garrison on the east side of North River.

REFERENCE: Willard's "Centennial Address," p. 95; Marvin's "History of Lancaster," p. 110-149-729-740; "American Ancestry," Vol. 9, p. 113.

68. Albert Judson Fisher.

HENRY HOUGHTON.—Soldier in the garrison commanded by Josiah Whitcomb at Lancaster during Queen Anne's War, 1704, composed of those who lived in Bolton, toward the northeast corner. Was himself in command of a garrison at Lancaster.

REFERENCE: Nourse's "Military Annals of Lancaster," p. 133; Nourse's "Early Records of Lancaster," p. 143-173; Mass Archives, Vol. 71, p. 876; Marvin's "History of Lancaster," p. 110.

68. Albert Judson Fisher.

THOMAS HOVEY.—[1648-1739]—Of Hadley. Lieutenant in King Philip's War.

REFERENCE: Savage's Genealogical Dictionary.

43. Harry Linn Wright.

JOHN HOW.—[—— 1687]—Sudbury, Mass., in 1638. Soldier in King Philip's War; in garrison in 1675.

REFERENCE: Society of Colonial Wars Year Book; Hudson's "History of Marlborough," p. 380-381; Hudson's "Annals of Sudbury, Wayland and Maynard," p. 22-253; Savage's Gen. Dictionary.

68. Albert Judson Fisher.

ISAAC HOWE.—Was appointed Ensign of First Company, or Train Band, at Stamford, Conn., in Oct., 1722; was also Ensign in 1732.

REFERENCE: Conn. Colonial Records, p. 331; Huntington Hist. Stamford, Conn., p. 185.

10. Edward Milton Adams.

JOSIAH HOWE, SR.—[—— 1711]—In Marlborough, Mass., in 1675, and "rallied with others to defend the inhabitants at the opening of King Philip's War."

REFERENCE: Hudson's "History of Marlborough," p. 380-381-385; Hudson's "Annals of Sudbury, Wayland and Maynard," Ed. 1891, p. 253.

 68. Albert Judson Fisher.

EDWARD HOWELL.—[1585-1656]—Lynn, Mass. Assistant 1647-53, Connecticut Colony.

REFERENCE: Society Colonial Wars Year Book, 1895.

 42. Charles Thomson Atkinson.

MAJOR JOHN HOWELL.—[1625-1695]—Southampton, L. I. Deputy, 1662-64. Commander Troop of Horse, 1684.

REFERENCE: Society Colonial Wars Year Book, 1895.

 42. Charles Thomson Atkinson.

THOMAS HOWES, SR.—Was a member of Capt. William Palmer's Military Company at Yarmouth, Mass., Aug., 1643.

REFERENCE: Pierce's Colonial Lists, p. 74.

 37. Frank Bassett Tobey.

THOMAS HOWES, JR.—[—— 1676]—Was Ensign at Yarmouth, Mass., 1672 to 1674; was promoted Captain June 3, 1674; was member of War Council, which controlled garrison at Yarmouth, Mass. Appointed April 2, 1667.

REFERENCE: Plymouth Col. Records, Vol. 5, p. 92-113-143-146-164-195-134.

 37. Frank Bassett Tobey.

JOHN HOWLAND.—[1593-1673]—Signer of Compact on the Mayflower. He was Assistant in Plymouth Colony, 1633-45, and as late as 1670 was serving as Deputy from Plymouth. Assistant to the Governor to raise soldiers, 1637

REFERENCE: Year Book, Society of Colonial Wars; Savage's Genealogical Dictionary; Davis' Ancient Landmarks of Plymouth.

 4. William Ruggles Tucker.
 5. John Smith Sargent.
 10. Edward Milton Adams.
 51. Franklin Adams Meacham.

THOMAS HUCKINS.—Of Barnstable. Member of Colonial War Council, June 5, 1671, to inaugurate campaign against Awashonk, the Squaw Sachem; was Commissary General of all Plymouth Colony forces in King Philip's War, 1675; was member of Barnstable Town War Council, Feb. 29, 1675.

REFERENCE: Pierce's Colonial Lists, p. 94-96-98; Plymouth Colonial Records; Society of Colonial Wars Year Book, 1895.

 50. Albert Eugene Snow.

DANIEL HUDSON.—[1697]—Of Lancaster. **Soldier in Capt. Joseph Sill's Company, King Philip's War; also in garrison at Lancaster, 1691-2.**
REFERENCE: N. E. Hist. and Gen. Reg., Vol. 41, p. 407; Vol. 43, p. 261.

    18. Scott Jordan.

LIEUTENANT CORNELIUS HULL.—Fairfield, Conn; messenger of the Council of War, Oct., 1675; appointed Lieutenant of the "Honored Major Treat's Life Guard," 1675, King Philip's War; Deputy from Fairfield to the General Court, 1676.
REFERENCE: Society of Colonial Wars Year Book, 1895, p. 238-239; Connecticut Colonial Records, Vol. 1665-1677, p. 411-378-279-327; also Vol. 1689-1706, p. 507; 1706-1716, p. 109-115-130.

    48. Henry Austin Osborn.

CAPTAIN THEOPHILUS HULL.—Ensign, 1705; Lieutenant, 1709; Captain, 1709, of the West Military Company of Fairfield, Conn.; member of the "Committee of War," Fairfield County, 1709.
REFERENCE: Society of Colonial Wars Year Book, 1895, p. 238-239; Connecticut Colonial Records, Vol. 1665-1677, p. 411-378-279-327; also Vol. 1689-1706, p. 507; Vol. 1706-1716, p. 109-115-130.

    48. Henry Austin Osborn.

SERGEANT JOHN HUMPHREY.—Was **Sergeant in the** Simsbury, Conn., Train Band. Simsbury, Conn., town records call him "Sergt.," Dec. 20, 1693.
REFERENCE: Simsbury Probate Records, Vol. 2, p 48; Simsbury Town Records (manuscript). Humphrey Genealogy, by F. Humphreys.

    10. Edward Milton Adams.
    33. Deming Haven Preston.

LIEUTENANT SAMUEL HUMPHREY.—Was Ensign, 1698; was Lieutenant, 1710; was Deputy from Simsbury, 1702, and later. Commissioned Lieutenant by Gov. Saltonstall, May, 1710.
REFERENCE: Mass. and Conn. Colonial Records; Humphrey Genealogy, by F. Humphrey.

    10. Edward Milton Adams.
    72. Lester Orestes Goddard.

EPHRAIM HUNT, JR.—Was Captain in the expedition to the St. Lawrence River, under Sir William Phipps in 1690; was given title for services then rendered, of Colonel. In expedition against Indians at Groton in 1706-7. He was also Governor's Councillor, or Assistant, from 1703 until **his death in** 1713. Appointed Ensign at Weymouth, Mass., March 16, 1680.
REFERENCE: Savage's Genealogical Dictionary; Ellis Genealogy, notes; History of Easton; Col. Records, 1674-86, p. 306; Pope Genealogy, p. 285.

    44. James Monroe Flower.

SAMUEL HUNT, JR.—[1657-1742-3]—Of Concord, Billerica and Tewksbury, Mass. Soldier in Capt. John Lane's Company of Militia, Major Jonathan Tyng's regiment, 1702, and participated in the march and rescue to the relief of Lancaster, Mass., against the French and Indians. His home near Wameset, now called Lowell, Mass., was used as a garrison during King William's War, 1689-1697, and also during Queen Anne's War, 1700-1712.

REFERENCE: History of Billerica, Mass., p. 75-76; Geneallogical Register of Billerica, report of Lieut.-Col. Jos. Lynde, dated Charlestown, Mass., Aug. 25, 1695; Court Records, Vol. 20, p. 444, and Vol. 16, p. 67; History of Connecticut Valley in Massachusetts, Vol. 2, Franklin Co., p. 687-688.

 2. Captain Philip Reade.

SAMUEL HUNT, SR.—[1633 ——]—of Agawam, now called Ipswich, Mass., in 1655, then of Billerica, Mass. Was a grantee of Bernardstown, Franklin Co., Mass., in reward of military service in the Falls Fight, also Deerfield, Mass., May 19, 1676. He was a soldier in Capt. William Turner's Company of Volunteers in King Philip's War. He was also a soldier under Maj. Samuel Appleton against the Narragansetts and participated in the Great Swamp Fight, Dec. 19, 1675.

REFERENCE: Savage's Genealogical Dictionary, Vol. 2, p. 502; History of Ipswich, Mass., p. 147-323; History of Billerica, Mass., p. 117-133-137.

 2. Captain Philip Reade.

WILLIAM HUNT.—[1605-1667]—Soldier in Capt. William Turner's Troop of Dorchester and Boston, April 7, 1676.

REFERENCE: Mass. Archives, Vol. 68, p. 21-195.

 2. Captain Philip Reade.

AMOS HURD.—He was a soldier in the old French wars called the Seven Years' War and perished of starvation in the campaign of 1759.

REFERENCE: Cothrens History of Ancient Woodbury; Society of Colonial Wars Register, 1894, p. 193.

 23. Alfred Beers Eaton.

JONATHAN HYDE.—Was in Capt. Thomas Wheeler's Co., scouting near Sudbury and Marlboro, King Philip's War. His name appears on roll, June 24, 1676.

REFERENCE: N. E. Hist. and Gen. Reg. Vol. 38, p. 42.

 52. Hobart Chatfield Chatfield-Taylor.

JOHN JENNEY.—Of Plymouth, was "Assistant" of Plymouth Colony, 1637-8-1640.

REFERENCE: Plymouth Colonial Records; Pierce's Colonial Lists, p. 4.

 50. Albert Eugene Snow.

EDWARD JOHNSON.—Was Captain of Woburn, Mass., Militia Company; charter member of A. & H. Artillery Company, Boston; Surveyor General of Arms for Mass., 1659; Deputy thirty times.

REFERENCE: Society of Colonial Wars Year Book, 1894, p. 126-185; Savage's Gen. Dict.

10. Edward Milton Adams.
51. Franklin Adams Meacham.

CAPTAIN ISAAC JOHNSON.—[—— 1675]—A member of the Artillery Company in 1645. Ensign of the Roxbury Military Company previous to 1653. Elected June 13, 1653, Captain of said company. Captain of Artillery Company in 1667. Representative to the General Court, 1671. Upon the mustering of the forces for Narragansett campaign he was placed in command of a company made up of men from Roxbury, Dorchester, Milton, Braintree, Weymouth, Hingham and Hull. Killed while leading his men across the fatal tree bridge at the entrance to the fort, Dec. 19, 1675.

REFERENCE: N. E. H. and G. Reg., Vol. 38, p. 280; Vol. 39, p. 74; Massachusetts Archives, Vol. 67, p. 45-219-226-293; Society of Colonial Wars Year Book, 1894, p. 39.

1. Seymour Morris.
47. Major Forrest Henry Hathaway.

JOHN JOHNSON.—[1600-1659]—Of Roxbury. A member of the first General Court in 1634, and for many years thereafter; a member of the Artillery Company in 1638; Surveyor General of arms and ammunition.

REFERENCE Society of Colonial Wars Year Book, 1894, p. 39; Savage's Gen. Dict., Mass. Bay Colonial Records, Vol. 1, p. 79; Vol. 2, p. 22-26-55-99-145-186-197-201-238-245-265; Vol. 4, part 1, p. 2-37-74-77-110-120-154-255-286-304-320-365.

1. Seymour Morris.
68. Albert Judson Fisher.

ANDREW JOHNSTONE.—[1694-1762]—Of Perth Amboy, N. J. Speaker of Provincial Assembly; for many years a member of the Governor's Council.

REFERENCE: Lamb's History of New York City; Appleton's Cyclopedia of American Biography; History of Trenton, N. J.; American Historical Register, Vol. 1, p. 1-2.

4. William Ruggles Tucker.

NATHANIEL JONES.—Captain. Representative to the General Court of Suffolk County, Mass., in 1727.

REFERENCE: Bond's History of Watertown; Reminiscences of Worcester, Mass.; Proprietary Records of Worcester, p. 283-264-251-244.

5. John Smith Sargent.

JOHN JUDD.—Ensign and Lieutenant, Farmington Train Band; Deputy from Farmington.

REFERENCE: Colonial Records of Connecticut, 1689-1706; p. 65-75-79-89, etc., p. 142-235-245-264-434.

    42. Charles Thomson Atkinson.

LIEUTENANT JOSEPH KELLOGG.—Of Farmington, Conn., Boston, and Hadley, Mass.; was Lieutenant in command of Hadley, Mass., troops in the Falls Fight, May 18, 1676. Sergeant in Capt. Wm. Turner's Company in the Falls Fight, May 19, 1676.

REFERENCE: Judd's History of Hadley, Mass.; Savage's Genealogical Dictionary; Society of Colonial Wars Year Book, 1895, p. 242.

    10. Edward Milton Adams.
    21. William Wolcott Strong.
    43. Harry Linn Wright.

HENRY KIMBALL.—Member of the quota of soldiers furnished by the Town of Haverhill, Mass., Bay Colony.

REFERENCE: History of Haverhill, p. 128.

    2. Captain Philip Reade.

ENSIGN JOHN LAKIN.—[—— 1697]—Ensign, 1692. Commander of garrison at Groton. Sergeant in King Philip's War.

REFERENCE: Society of Colonial Wars Year Book, 1895, p. 243.

    26. Horatio Loomis Wait.

MAJOR JOB LANE.—[1624-1697]—Malden, Mass., 1654. Billerica, 1664. During King Philip's War had a garrison against Indians. Representative to General Court, 1674, 1680 and 1685.

REFERENCE: Society of Colonial Wars Year Book; Hazen's "History of Billerica," p. 88 of Appendix 3, 139-176; Mass. Bay Colonial Records, Vol. 3, p. 99-261-393-476; the Reyner family; the Lane family.

    68. Albert Judson Fisher.
    70. Charles Ridgely.

COLONEL JOHN LANE.—[1661-1715]—Lieutenant of the Billerica Troop, 1693, King William's War. Captain of the same, 1699. Major of the West Regiment of Horse and Foot, 1711, Queen Anne's War. Deputy to the General Court, 1702. Colonel of Massachusetts Militia. Died in the service.

REFERENCE: S. C. W. Year Book, 1895, p. 243.

    73. Anthony French Merrill.

CAPTAIN DANIEL LAWRENCE.—[1681-1777]—Of Groton, Mass., and Plainfield, Conn., May, 1736. Commissioned Captain of the First Company or Train Band of Plainfield, Conn.; was Deputy from Plainfield to General Court eleven times between 1722 and 1741.

REFERENCE: Colonial Records of Connecticut, Vol. 8, p. 32; Dr. R. M. Lawrence's "Historical Sketches of the Lawrence Family," p. 42-43.

18. Scott Jordan.

ENOCH LAWRENCE.—[1648-9-1744]—Of Watertown and Groton. A soldier in King Philip's War; also in Groton Garrison, 1691-2; was badly wounded in a fight with Indians, July 27, 1694, King William's War.

REFERENCE: N. E. Hist. and Gen. Reg., Vol. 43, p. 274-374; Dr. S. A. Greene's "Groton During the Indian Wars," p. 84-85; Historical Sketches of the Lawrence family, p. 38-39; Massachusetts Archives, Vol. 70, p. 583.

18. Scott Jordan.

ENSIGN THOMAS LEE.—Ensign of the Lyme Train Band, 1701; Deputy to the General Court, 1676, of the Colony of Connecticut.

REFERENCE: Society of Colonial Wars Year Book, 1895, p. 24.

71. Ebenezer Lane.

GOVERNOR WILLIAM LEETE.—Governor of Connecticut, 1661 to 1665, and again, 1677 to 1683; was Assistant, 1669 and 1643 to 1657. Deputy Governor, 1658-76; was Commissioner to United Colonies, 1655 to 1679.

REFERENCE: Society of Colonial Wars Year Book, 1894, p. 42.

10. Edward Milton Adams.

ENSIGN THOMAS LEFFINGWELL.—Ensign in 1701; Deputy, 1716.

REFERENCE: Conn. Colonial Records, Vol. 3.

70. Charles Ridgely.
71. Ebenezer Lane.

LIEUTENANT THOMAS LEFFINGWELL.—Ensign in 1657; Lieutenant of the Norwich County Train Band, 1672; served in King Philip's War; also served in Capt. Denison's famous band of Indian fighters. Deputy to the General Court, 1671-1710.

REFERENCE: Society of Colonial Wars Year Book, 1895, p. 245.

70. Charles Ridgely.
71. Ebenezer Lane.

JOHN LEONARD—Of Springfield, Mass., 1639. He was killed by the Indians in King Philip's War early in 1676.

REFERENCE: Savage's Gen. Dict.; Judd's History of Hadley, Mass.; N. E. Hist. and Gen. Register, Vol. 40, p. 212; History of W. Mass., Vol. 2, p. 318.

60. John Conant Long.
68. Albert Judson Fisher.

LIEUTENANT JAMES LEWIS.—[1637-1713]—Lieutenant of Barnstable Company.

REFERENCE: Society of Colonial Wars Year Book, 1895, p. 246.

15. Josiah Lewis Lombard.

SAMUEL LEWIS.—Was Sergeant. Farmington, Conn., 1676.

REFERENCE: Savage's Genealogical Dictionary, N. E.

42. Charles Thomson Atkinson.

CAPTAIN WILLIAM LEWIS.—A Sergeant and Captain in the Narragansett campaign, King Philip's War, 1675; Sergeant, May 17, 1649; Lieutenant, Oct. 6, 1651; Captain, Oct. 8, 1674. Captain of the Farmington, Conn., Train Band in 1674; Deputy, 1689-90.

REFERENCE: Savage's Genealogical Dictionary of New England, Vol. III, p. 89; Connecticut Colonial Records, Vol. 1636-1665, pp. 187, 227, 300. Vol. 1665, 1677, pp. 101 and 238. Society of Colonial Wars Year Book, 1895, p. 246.

33. Deming Haven Preston.
42. Charles Thomson Atkinson.
59. Charles Pratt Whitney.

ROBERT LONG.—Charlestown, Mass.; a member of the Ancient and Honorable Artillery Company, of Boston, 1639.

REFERENCE: Savage's Genealogical Dictionary.

1. Seymour Morris.
28. Cyrus Austin Hardy.
52. Hobart Chatfield Chatfield-Taylor.

CAPTAIN RICHARD LORD.—[1611-1662]—Was Captain of the First Troop of Horse, Colony of Conn., 1657. One of the patentees under the charter of 1662 from Charles II.

REFERENCE: Society of Colonial Wars Year Book, 1895, p. 248.

7. Edward McKinstry Teall.

LIEUTENANT RICHARD LORD.—[1669-1712]—Was Treasurer of the Colony of Connecticut, elected Jan. 14, 1712. He was elected Auditor, 1706; Lieutenant, May, 1700; on Committee on War, 1708.

REFERENCE: Connecticut Colonial Records for 1689 to 1716.

7. Edward McKinstry Teall.

CAPTAIN EBENEZER LOTHROP.—Commissioned Ensign in First Train Band, Norwich, Conn., 1740; Lieutenant in 1742; Captain in 1745.

REFERENCE: Connecticut Colonial Records.

70. Charles Ridgely.

CAPTAIN SAMUEL LOTHROP.—Served at Port Royal in 1710. Commissioned Ensign in 1721, Fourth Train Band of Connecticut; in 1724 commissioned Captain of Second Train Band.

REFERENCE: Colonial Records, Vol. 3, pp. 235-446.

70. Charles Ridgely.

JUDGE SAMUEL LOTHROP.—When, in 1657, Uncas routed by the Narragansetts, had been chased into the fort at the head of the Nahantic and was there besieged, Lieut. James Avery, Mr. Brewster, Samuel Lothrop and others succeeded in throwing themselves into the fort and aided in the defense.

REFERENCE: Lothrop Family Memoir.

65. Joseph Lathrop.
70. Charles Ridgely.

DANIEL LOVETT.—Was Lieutenant, 1730; Captain, 1735; Major, 1743, at Mendon, Mass.

REFERENCE: See Annals of Mendon, copying town records, pp. 216, 227, 246, 253.

10. Edward Milton Adams.
51. Franklin Adams Meacham.

JAMES LOVETT.—Of Mendon, Mass. Was Sergeant, 1689; Ensign, 1693; Lieutenant, 1710; Captain later.

REFERENCE: Annals of Mendon, copying town records, pp. 106, 117, 121, 159 and later.

10. Edward Milton Adams.
51. Franklin Adams Meacham.

WILLIAM LUMPKIN.—A private in the Yarmouth, Mass., Company.

REFERENCE: Pierce's Colonial Lists, p. 74.

15. Josiah Lewis Lombard.
32. Rev. James Gibson Johnson.
63. Rev. Abbott Eliot Kittredge.

FRANCIS LYFORD.—[1645-1723]—A private in Capt. Kinsley Hall's Company of Exeter, N. H., in King William's War.

REFERENCE: Bell's History of Exeter, N. H.

39. George Samuel Marsh.

LIEUTENANT JOHN LYMAN.—He was in command of the Northampton soldiers in the famous Falls Fight above Deerfield, May 18, 1676. Capt. William Turner, under whom he served, was killed.

REFERENCE: Lyman Genealogy, p. 40. New England Historical and Genealogical Register, Vol. 41, pp. 201 to 218.

6. Lyman Dresser Hammond.
54. William Ward Wight.

LIEUTENANT GEORGE MACEY.—Of Taunton. Ensign, ——. Promoted to Lieutenant, June, 1665; promoted Captain, April, 1690; made Associate Judge, June, 1690; was member of Capt. Poole's Co., of Taunton, 1643, was Lieutenant from Taunton, Mass., King Philip's War; Deputy Plymouth Colony, 1672-78.

REFERENCE. Plymouth Colony Records, Vol. IV, p. 93; Vol. VI, p. 237; Pierce's Colonial Lists, pp. 75; Savage's Gen. Dict.; Baylie's New Plymouth; Society of Colonial Wars Year Book, 1895.

45. Francis Porter Fisher.

ONESIPHOROUS MARSH, SR.—[1630-1713]—Of Haverhill, Mass. Member of the Militia Company under Capt. William White, in 1662. He was in command of and owned one of the small garrison forts built by the town in King Philip's War, 1675. During King William's War, 1684-1697, he was a member of one of the town garrisons, commanded by Sergeant Haseltine.

REFERENCE: Town Records, p. 117; Savage, Vol. III, p. 154; History of Essex Co., Mass.; History of Haverhill; Sewall's Diary.

2. Captain Philip Reade.

CAPTAIN HUGH MASON.—[1605-1678]—Of Watertown. Deputy to the General Court of Mass. nine times, 1635-77. Commander in Chief, 1664; member of the Council of War, 1676; Lieutenant and Captain of the Train Band of Watertown, Mass., 1652; in command of the Watertown Militia in the Sudbury fight, King Philip's War, April 21, 1676.

REFERENCE: Society of Colonial Wars Year Book, 1894, pp. 76, 174, 183, 189 and 210.

25. Judge Frank Baker.

MAJOR JOHN MASON.—Lieutenant under Sir Thomas Fairfax in the Netherlands; Representative to General Court, 1635-1641; Deputy Governor, 1659-1669; Commissioner to the United Colonies for five sessions, 1647-1661; commanded forces in Pequot War.

REFERENCE: Sparks' American Biography, Vol. III; Year Book, 1894; Society of Colonial Wars, p. 47.

42. Charles Thomson Atkinson.

JOHN MAYO.—A member of the "Barnstable Company" of Plymouth Colony, Lieutenant Thomas Dymoke commanding. Active service in 1643-44.

REFERENCE: Society of Colonial Wars Year Book, 1895, p. 253.

15. Josiah Lewis Lombard.
32. Rev. James Gibson Johnson.
63. Rev. Abbott Eliot Kittredge.

SAMUEL MAYO.—A member of the "Barnstable Company" of Plymouth Colony, Lieutenant Thomas Dymoke commanding. Active service in 1643-44.

REFERENCE: Society of Colonial Wars Year Book, 1895, p. 253; Pierce's Colonial Lists, p. 73.

15. Josiah Lewis Lombard.
32. Rev. James Gibson Johnson.
63. Rev. Abbott Eliot Kittredge.

LIEUTENANT JAMES M'DOWELL.—[1716 ——]—Of Augusta Co., Va. Was Lieutenant of an Augusta County, Va., company in the French and Indian War, 1754-63. Lieut. James McDowell, of Augusta County (Va.) Militia, received arrears of pay, by order of the General Assembly, Sept., 1758."

REFERENCE: Thos. Marshall Green's "Historic Families of Kentucky," 1st Series, pp. 12, 13; Hening's "Statutes at Large," Vol. VII, p. 195.

18. Scott Jordan.

JOHN MOHR M'INTOSH.—Settled at New Iverness, Ga. (now Darien) on the Albemarle. John Mohr McIntosh entered actively upon the defense of the Colony against the Spaniards. He was appointed Captain of a Highland company, the first in America. He was in command of this company during Gen. Oglethorpe's operations to capture St. Augustine from the Spaniards in 1740. He was the founder of McIntosh County and the County was named for him.

REFERENCE: Historical Register of Officers of the Continental Army, p. 278; Appleton's Cyclopedia of American Biography, Vol. 4, p. 124.

9. Frederick Hampden Winston.

CAPTAIN SAMUEL MEREDITH.—[1732-1808]—Captain in Col. Wm. Byrd's Regiment. Served at Forts Chiswell, Cumberland, Pitt, etc.

REFERENCE: Society of Colonial Wars Year Book, 1895, pp. 253-83 and 166.

74. Hiram Holbrook Rose.

WILLIAM MERRICK.—Was a member of the Duxbury Company of Plymouth Colony, under Capt. Myles Standish, in active service, 1642-1644. He was an Ensign at Eastham, Cape Cod, Mass. Was promoted to be Lieutenant, June, 1663.

REFERENCE: Pierce's Colonial Lists; Society Colonial Wars Year Book, 1895; Plymouth Colonial Records, Vol. IV, p. 41.

58. Frederick Laforrest Merrick.

NATHANIEL MERRIMAN.—Sergeant in Train Band at New Haven, on July —, 1665; promoted Lieutenant at Wallingford, Ct., May, 1672; promoted Captain of troop of dragoons for New Haven County, Nov. 1, 1675.

REFERENCE: Connecticut Colonial Records, Vol. 1665-1677, pp. 23, 172, 379.

59. Charles Pratt Whitney.

THOMAS MINOR.—Was Lieutenant from Stonington, Conn. Was Deputy, 1650-51-65-70-73.

REFERENCE: Conn. Colonial Records; Savage's Genealogical Dictionary.

10. Edward Milton Adams.
51. Franklin Adams Meacham.

ENSIGN JACOB MITCHELL.—Of Bridgewater, Mass. Killed King Philip's War, 1675.

REFERENCE: Mitchell's Bridgewater.

72. Lester Orestes Goddard.

LIEUTENANT JOHN MOFFETT.—[1708-1744]—Of Augusta Co., Va. "On June 24, 1742, John Moffett qualified as Lieutenant of Militia at the Orange County (Va.) Court."
REFERENCE: "Early Records of Orange Co. (Va.) Court," p. 396; Annals of Augusta Co., Va., 1888 Edition.

18. Scott Jordan.

WILLIAM MONROE.—[1669-1759]—Of Lexington. Ensign of Militia.
REFERENCE: Hudson History of Lexington, pp. 149.

25. Frank Baker.

ENSIGN JOHN MOORE.—[—— 1702]—Sudbury and Lancaster, Mass. Appointed Sergeant of Lancaster Company, April 20, 1670; elected its Ensign July 3, 1689; served in garrison at Lancaster, 1676, and after; Representative to the General Court, 1689-1690; Selectman, 1690. Died Sept., 1702.
REFERENCE: Nourse's "Military Annals of Lancaster," p. 9; Nourse's "Early Records of Lancaster," pp. 125, 128, 133; Marvin's "History of Lancaster," pp. 61-110; Willard's "Centennial Address," p. 95.

68. Albert Judson Fisher.

JOHN MOORE, SR.—[—— 1703]—Sudbury and Lancaster, Mass. At Sudbury, 1638, or earlier. Probably of Ancient and Honorable Artillery Co., 1638. Served in garrison of Lawrence Waters following the attack of King Philip's 1,500 warriors upon Lancaster, Feb. 10, 1676. Representative to the General Court, 1689 to 1692.
REFERENCE: Savage's Genealogical Dictionary; Hudson's "Annals of Sudbury, Wayland and Maynard," pp. 2, 201, 204; Marvin's "History of Lancaster," p. 110; Whitman's "History of A. & H. Artillery Co."; Willard's "Centennial Address," p. 95; Nourse's "Early Records of Lancaster," pp. 128, 333.

68. Albert Judson Fisher.

JONATHAN MOORE.—[1669-1742]—He and his brother John had a garrison during Queen Anne's War, 1704, at Lancaster, Mass.
REFERENCE: Nourse's "Early Records of Lancaster," pp. 143-306; Mass. Archives, LXXI, 876; Marvin's "History of Lancaster," pp. 110-138.

68. Albert Judson Fisher.

DAVID MORGAN.—One of the defenders of Springfield, Mass., at its burning by the Indians during King Philip's War.
REFERENCE: History of Springfield, pp. 162, 165, by Mason A. Greene; Savage's Genealogical Dictionary; Morris' "Burning of Springfield"; Appendix, p. 74.

68. Albert Judson Fisher.

CAPTAIN MILES MORGAN.—[1616-1699]—Of Springfield, Mass. An old Indian hunter. For many years Sergeant and afterward Captain of the military company of Springfield. Capt. Morgan built a block-house and stockade, which he and his five sons ably defended against the Indians.

REFERENCE: American Ancestry, Vol. 3, p. 36; History of Brimfield; History of Springfield, p. 126, by M. A. Greene.

68. Albert Judson Fisher.

LIEUTENANT EDWARD MORRIS.—[1630-1689]—Of Roxbury, Mass., and Woodstock, Conn. Representative to the General Court from Roxbury, 1677-1687; founder of the town of Woodstock, Conn., in 1686, and their first military officer.

REFERENCE: Savage's Genealogical Dictionary; Year Book; Society of Colonial Wars; Larned's History of Windham County, Conn.

1. Seymour Morris.
6. Lyman Dresser Hammond.

LIEUTENANT EDWARD MORRIS.—[1688-1769]—Of Woodstock, Conn.; Lieutenant of the Woodstock Company.

REFERENCE: Savage's Genealogical Dictionary; Morris' Register; Larned's History of Windham County, Conn.

1. Seymour Morris.

LIEUTENANT JOHN MOSELEY.—[1640-1690]—Lieutenant in the Westfield Company of Foot in King Philip's War.

REFERENCE: Society of Colonial Wars Year Book, 1895, p. 256.

54. William Ward Wight.

LIEUTENANT SAMUEL NASH.—Of Duxbury Company prior to 1683; was private to Lieut. Wm. Holmes Company against Pequot Indians, 1637; Sheriff of Plymouth Colony, 1652; Chief Marshal of General Court, 1652; Deputy to General Court from Duxbury, 1653; Member of Council of War, 1658.

REFERENCE: Plymouth Colony Records; Savage's Dictionary.

46. George Butters.

BENJAMIN NEWBERRY.—Was a Captain in King Philip's War.

REFERENCE: Baldwin's Candee Genealogy, p. 127; Wight's The Wights, pp. 225-226; Savage's Dictionary.

54. William Ward Wight.

SOCIETY OF COLONIAL WARS

LIEUTENANT ANDREW NEWCOMB.—Was chosen Lieutenant at Edgartown, Mass., April 13, 1691. Was in command of the fortification there, having such number of men under him as were ordered by the Chief Magistrate.

REFERENCE: New York Colonial Records, Vol. 37, p. 230; Town Records of Edgartown, Vol. 1, p. 38.

38. George Whitfield Newcomb.

ROBERT PADDOCK.—Was a member of the Military Company at Plymouth, Mass., 1643.

REFERENCE: Pierce's Colonial Lists, p. 76.

37. Frank Bassett Tobey.

JOHN PAEBODIE.—[1590-1667]—A member of the Duxbury Military Company under Capt. Myles Standish in August, 1643.

REFERENCE: Pierce's Colonial Lists, p. 75.

4. William Ruggles Tucker.

BRINTON PAINE.—[1741-1820]—Served in Capt. Saml. Chapman's Company from Bolton, Conn., in the French and Indian War.

REFERENCE: Waldo's Early History of Tolland, Conn., p. 45.

7. Edward McKinstry Teall.

STEPHEN PAINE.—[1654-1710]—Of Rehoboth, Mass., 1675. A soldier in King Philip's War and a large contributor to the expense thereof.

REFERENCE: Paine Genealogy.

7. Edward McKinstry Teall.

THOMAS PAINE.—Of Plymouth and Yarmouth. Member of Yarmouth Military Company, 1643; under command of Lieut. Wm. Palmer; Deputy from Yarmouth, 1639.

REFERENCE: Pierce's Colonial Lists, p. 74; Plymouth Colonial Records.

15. Josiah Lewis Lombard.
18. Scott Jordan.
58. Frederick Laforrest Merrick.

ICHABOD PALMER.—Of Stonington, Conn. Was Ensign, Oct., 1737; Lieutenant, 1739.

REFERENCE: Connecticut Colonial Records, 1735; pp. 43, 120, 261.

10. Edward Milton Adams.
51. Franklin Adams Meacham.

NEHEMIAH PALMER.—Of Stonington, Conn., was Governor's Councillor, 1703. Deputy many years. Was Deputy for Stonington to Conn. General Court, 1668, and many times thereafter.

REFERENCE: Connecticut Colonial Records, 1689-1706, pp. 212.

10. Edward Milton Adams.
51. Franklin Adams Meacham.

ROBERT PARISH.—Of Groton and Dunstable, Mass. Was a soldier in Captain Samuel Moseley's Independent Company of Volunteers and served under Major Samuel Appleton, commanding the Mass. forces under Josiah Winslow, Commander in Chief of the Army against the Narragansetts, King Philip's War. He was a member of the garrison, Dunstable, Mass., Aug. 24 to Sept. 23, 1676, and at other times during King Philip's War. He was also a member of Jonathan Tyng's garrison at Dunstable in 1689, King William's War. He was also in local military service, Dunstable, Mass., during the early portion of Queen Anne's War.

REFERENCE: Reprint from Pay rolls of Mr. John Hull, Treasurer at War, Mass. Bay Colony; "Soldiers in King Philip's War;" N. E. H. & G. Reg., Vol. 37, p. 182; also Vol. 43, p. 263; Mass. Archives, Vol. CVII, p. 230, Vol. LXXI, p. 83; History of Dunstable, Mass.

2. Captain Philip Reade.

SURGEON THOMAS PARISH.—Was surgeon in Captain George Cooke's Co. in the expedition ordered on foot against Samuel Gurton in 1643.

REFERENCE: Massachusetts Colonial Records, Vol. 2, pp. 53, 346; Savage's Genealogical Dictionary, Vol. 3.

2. Captain Philip Reade.

WILLIAM PARKE.—Was member of A. & H. Artillery Co., Boston, 1638.

REFERENCE: Savage's Genealogical Dictionary; Whitman's Artillery Co., p. 148.

52. Hobart Chatfield Chatfield-Taylor.

MAJOR JOHN PELL.—[1643-1702]—Second Lord of the Manor of Pelham; Member of New York Provincial Assembly for Westchester County, 1691-95; Captain of Horse, Provincial Forces, New York, 1684; Major, 1692, French and Indian War.

REFERENCE: Society of Colonial Wars Year Book, 1894; Bolton's History of Westchester; New York State Records.

12. Rodman Corse Pell.

SERGEANT JOHN PERKINS.—[1590-1654]—Was Sergeant of the Allied English and the friendly aboriginal Indians under their Chief Masconoma, at Agawam (Ipswich, Mass., Bay Colony), during the war with the Tarratines, July to September, 1631.

REFERENCE: Town Records of Ipswich; History of Ipswich, History of Essex Co., Mass., p. 200; and Gov. John Winthrop's Journal.

2. Captain Philip Reade.

ARTHUR PERRY.—Of Boston, 1630.—Member of the Ancient and Honorable Artillery Company, 1638.

REFERENCE: Savage's Genealogical Dictionary.

7. Edward McKinstry Teall.

WILLIAM PHELPS.—Was Representative to the First General Court in Mass., Assistant in 1634; removed to Windsor, Conn., 1635; Assistant in 1636 and 1658.

REFERENCE: Savage's Gen. Dict.; Connecticut Colonial Records.

45. Francis Porter Fisher.

JONATHAN PHINNEY.—Ensign of Windsor, Conn.

REFERENCE: Stiles' Windsor.

72. Lester Orestes Goddard.

CAPTAIN MICHAEL PIERCE.—Dec. 17, 1673, was chosen Ensign in Capt. James Endworth's Company. In 1669 commissioned Captain by the Colony Court. Was in the Great Swamp Fight, Dec. 19, 1675. After the Narragansett alarm of 1676 he was in command of the garrison of Seaconecke. Was sent to fight the hostile Indians near Pawtucket under Canonchet, having command of 50 Englishmen and 20 friendly Indians at Attleboro Gore.

REFERENCE: Pierce Genealogy.

41. John Larkin Lincoln, Jr.

SERGEANT NATHANIEL PINNEY.—Was in Captain Moses Dimond's Company of Windsor, Conn., men in the year 1711 in the expedition against Canada (Queen Anne's War, 1702-1713.)

REFERENCE: Manuscript Commissary Account of Roger Wolcott, State Archives of Connecticut; Stiles' Windsor.

72. Lester Orestes Goddard.

NATHANIEL PITKIN.—Was appointed Ensign at East Hartford May, 1716.

REFERENCE: Pitkin Genealogy; Connecticut Colonial Records, Vol. V., p. 550.

45. Francis Porter Fisher.

WILLIAM PITKIN.—Settled in Hartford about 1665; King's attorney, 1664; was Governor's Assistant, 1690 until death, 1694; Deputy, 1675-1690; Freeman, 1676; Commissioner for Connecticut to United Colonies.

REFERENCE: Pitkin Genealogy; Connecticut Colonial Records; Society of Colonial Wars Year Book, 1895.

45. Francis Porter Fisher.

CAPTAIN JONATHAN POOLE.—Of Reading, Mass. Ensign of the "Three County Troops," a Cavalry Company, in 1658. The flag of this troop was the first one designed and floated by the English Colonists in America, and Jonathan Poole was the standard bearer of this historic ensign. In King Philip's War he had a separate command of a company of foot soldiers doing duty as scouts. He was under Major Appleton at Hadley and was President of a Council of War in the winter of 1675-6.

REFERENCE: Drake, pp. 417.

57. Charles Clarence Poole.

THOMAS POPE.—Of Plymouth, was member of Volunteer Company from Plymouth, June 7, 1637, which, under Lieut. William Holmes and Thos. Prence, marched against Pequot Indians. He was also member of Military Co. at Plymouth in Aug., 1643.

REFERENCE: Pierce's Colonial Lists, pp. 9-84; Plymouth Colonial Records, Vol. 1, p. 61.

50. Albert Eugene Snow.

MOSES PORTER.—Enlisted in 1755 as a volunteer from the Colony of Massachusetts in the expedition planned by General Braddock against Crown Point. Captain of a Company from Hadley, Mass. In "Bloody Morning Scout," on Sept. 8, 1755, Capt. Porter was killed.

REFERENCE: "Montcalm and Wolfe," Vol. 1; History of Hadley, Mass.; Savage's Genealogical Dictionary.

45. Francis Porter Fisher.

ABRAHAM PREBLE.—Was Governor's Assistant to Sir Fernando Georges at Falmouth (now Portland), Maine, 1645 to 1649; was Major of the military forces at that place under Edward Godfrey; was Assistant under Deputy Governor Henry Joselin, July 6, 1646; was authorized by Mass. to grant military commissions after 1652.

REFERENCE: New England Hist. & Gene. Register, Vol. XXII, pp. 212-15; "Preble Family in America," p. 96; Mass. Colonial Records; also N. E. Hist. & Gene. Register, Vol. 7, p. 134, quoting York Co. Records.

 10. Edward Milton Adams.

GOVERNOR THOMAS PRENCE.—[1600-1678]—Governor of Plymouth Colony, 1635-1638-1658; Assistant many times. Member of Council of War and went forth against Pequot Indians in 1637; Commissioner for the United Colonies, 1645-50-61.

REFERENCE: Savage's Genealogical Dictionary; Freeman's History of Cape Cod; Plymouth Colony Records, 1635-1658.

 10. Edward Milton Adams.
 50. Albert Eugene Snow.
 51. Franklin Adams Meacham.
 58. Frederick Laforrest Merrick.
 61. Victor Clifton Alderson.

SOLOMON PRENTICE.—Served as soldier in Cambridge Company in King Philip's War.

REFERENCE: Account Book of Treasurer Hall in Library of N. E. H. G. Society; Mass. Archives, Vol. 68, pp. 73, 79 and 80.

 31. Charles Newton Fessenden.

JOHN PRESCOTT.—Served in garrison at Lancaster, Mass., and in defense of the town against Indians Aug. 22, 1675, and Feb. 10, 1676.

REFERENCE: Society of Colonial Wars Year Book, 1895, p. 265.

 1. Seymour Morris.
 14. Henry Sherman Boutell.
 24. Lemuel Ruggles Hall.

CAPTAIN JONATHAN PRESCOTT.—Of Watertown, Lancaster and Concord, Mass., was Captain of the Concord Militia in King Philip's War. His house was fortified as a garrison house in 1676.

REFERENCE: Prescott Genealogy, p. 42; N. E. H. & G. Register, Vol. 38, p. 42.

 14. Henry Sherman Boutell.
 24. Lemuel Ruggles Hall.

GENERAL ISRAEL PUTNAM.—At the outbreak of the French War, 1755, he raised a company of men in his neighborhood (Pomfret, Ct.); was appointed Captain in Lyman's Regiment; took part in the operation around Lake George and Crown Point; was promoted to rank of Major 1757. In 1758 was taken prisoner by the Indians. In 1759 became Lieut. Colonel and took an important part under Gen. Amheray in the Canadian Campaign.

REFERENCE: Connecticut Colonial Records, Vol. 1751-1757, pp. 399, 472, 539, 2, 601; Vol. 1757-1762, pp. 97, 226, 228, 356, 484, 618; Vol. 1762-1767, pp. 234, 249; Vol. 1772-1775, pp. 331, 423, 425.

   30. Chas. Durkee Dana.

LIEUTENANT NATHANIEL PUTNAM.—[1619-1700]—Lieutenant of the Foot Company of Salem Village, 1683; Deputy to the Massachusetts General Court, 1690-91.

REFERENCE: Year Book, Society of Colonial Wars, 1894, pp. 122-186.

   2. Captain Philip Reade.

THOMAS PUTNAM.—Was Lieutenant of Troop of Horse in Lynn, Mass., in 1662; served in King Philip's War.

REFERENCE: Society of Colonial Wars Year Book, 1895, p. 266; Putnam Genealogy; History of Lynn.

   5. John Smith Sargent.
   30. Charles Durkee Dana.

WILLIAM PYNCHON.—[1590-1662]—Of Springfield, Mass. Chartered Incorporator and "Assistant" Treasurer, 1632-1634. Governor of Springfield, 1641-1650. Governing Magistrate of Connecticut, 1637-1638.

REFERENCE: Society of Colonial Wars Year Book, 1895, p. 266.

   7. Edward McKinstry Teall.

JOHN REED.—[1704-1771]—Lieutenant in French and Indian Wars, 1756.

REFERENCE: "Seth Read, His ancestors and descendants," by M. R. Breford, 1895, p. 16.

   21. William Wolcott Strong.

JOHN REYNER.—Plymouth, Mass., 1636. Pastor Plymouth Church. Member Plymouth Military Company; Muster Roll, dated August, 1643; Will, dated Exeter, Mass., Jan. 30, 1669.

REFERENCE: Pierce's Colonial Lists, p. 76; Savage's Genealogical Dict.; "Lane Family;" "Reyner Family;" N. E. Hist. & Gen. Reg., Vol. XI, pp. 105-106.

   68. Albert Judson Fisher.

HENRY RHOADES.—Fought against the Indians in the Nipmuck country; was also in "Swamp Fight," 1675.
REFERENCE: Society of Colonial Wars Year Book, 1894, p. 206.

10. Edward Milton Adams.

SAMUEL RHOADES.—Was private in Captain Ebenezer Cox's Co. from Stoughtonham, Mass., in French and Indian War, 1760. Was in Samuel Miller's Regiment at Crown Point, April to December, 1756. Was in Capt. Nathaniel Blake's Company at Crown Point, May, 1756, to March, 1757.
REFERENCE: Hunton's History Canton, Mass., pp. 641, quoting from Mass. Archives.

10. Edward Milton Adams.

EDWARD RICE.—Owned Garrison house at Marlboro, Mass. Was member of West Middlesex Regiment and quartered in his Garrison house March 18, 1691.
REFERENCE: N. E. H. & G. Reg., Vol. 43, p. 372.

17. Frederick Clifton Pierce.

SAMUEL RICE.—Was member of the garrison at the house of Joseph Rice in Marlboro, Mass., in Oct., 1675.
REFERENCE: Mass. Archives, Vol. 67, p. 277; N. E Hist. & Gen. Reg., Vol. 40, pp. 315-16.

62. William Dorrance Messinger.

LIEUTENANT JOSIAH RICHARDSON.—[1665-1711]—Of Chelmsford, Mass. Lieutenant in West Regiment of Middlesex. Served in garrison at Chelmsford, March 16, 1691-2, during King William's War.
REFERENCE: New England Historical & Genealogical Register, Vol. 43, p. 372. Original Roll of West Regt. of Middlesex, Mass.; Memorial of the Richardson Family.

2. Captain Philip Reade.

NATHANIEL RICHARDSON.—[1651-1714]—Of Woburn, Mass.; private in Captain Prentiss' Company in the Great Swamp Fight, Dec. 19, 1675, where he was wounded.
REFERENCE: New England Historical and Genealogical Register, Vol. 37, p. 282.

1. Seymour Morris.

THOMAS ROBERTS.—Came with Hilton, 1623. Was last Colonial Governor of New Hampshire; elected April, 1640.
REFERENCE: Provincial Records of New Hampshire, Vol. 1, p. 119; Savage's Genealogical Dictionary, Vol. 3, p. 547; N. E. Hist. & Gene. Reg., Vol. 7, p. 356.

15. Josiah Lewis Lombard.

JOHN ROGERS.—A member of Capt. Myles Standish's Company of Duxbury, Mass., in August, 1643.

REFERENCE: Pierce's Colonial Lists, p. 75.

 4. William Ruggles Tucker.

JOHN RUGGLES.—Of Roxbury, Mass. Was in Captain Nicholas Manning's Company April 24, 1676. Was also in Lieutenant Gillams' Company under Major Savage. Was also Trooper under Captain Davis Jan., 1675. Was Deputy, 1658-60-61 and later.

REFERENCE: See copy of Hull's pay roll in New E. H. & G. Reg., Vol. 42, p. 95; Also Vol. 37, pp. 368-375; Massachusetts Archives, Vol. 68.

 10. Edward Milton Adams.
 24. Lemuel Ruggles Hall.
 49. Frank Eugene Spooner.

CAPTAIN SAMUEL RUGGLES.—Of Roxbury, Mass., was Deputy four years, Captain Roxbury Militia.

REFERENCE: Mass. Colonial Records, 1654-86, p. 73.

 4. William Ruggles Tucker.
 24. Lemuel Ruggles Hall.

BRIGADIER GENERAL TIMOTHY RUGGLES.—[1711-1795]—Of Rochester and Hardwick, Mass. Brigadier General and second in command at Lake George, 1755. President of Stamp Act Congress, N. Y., in 1765.

REFERENCE: Appleton's Cyclopedia of American Biography; Society of Colonial Wars Year Book.

 4. William Ruggles Tucker.

RICHARD SALTONSTALL.—[1610-1694]—Sergeant Major of Colonel Endicott's Regiment, Oct. 7, 1641. Assistant and Deputy to the General Court of Massachusetts Bay Colony, 1635-49.

REFERENCE: Society of Colonial Wars Year Book, 1895, p. 270.

 54. William Ward Wight.

HENRY SAMPSON.—[D. 1684]—Came in ship Mayflower, 1620. Private in Lieut. William Holmes' Company against Pequot Indians, 1637.

REFERENCE: Plymouth Colonial Records, Vol. 1; Giles Memorial.

 46. George Butters.

ZABDIEL SAMPSON.—[1727-1776]—Private from Duxbury in French War, 1756; taken prisoner and bound to a tree, a target for Indian amusement with hatchets. Released and was killed in War of Revolution.

REFERENCE: Giles Memorial, by Vinton, p. 400; Davis' Landmarks of Plymouth, p. 229.

46. George Butters.

THOMAS SAVERY.—Of Scituate; enlisted in Capt. Michael Pierce's Company; was killed by Indians in fight against Chief Canonchet, March 26, 1676.

REFERENCE: History of Plymouth Co., p. 412; Davis' Landmarks of Plymouth, p. 231.

46. George Butters.

WILLIAM SAWYER.—[1603-1702]—Of Woburn, Mass. Soldier under Major Samuel Appleton of Massachusetts at the Great Swamp Fight, Dec. 19, 1675.

REFERENCE: Soldiers of King Philip's War, 1675-7, p. 108; Massachusetts Archives, Vol. 68, p. 104.

2. Captain Philip Reade.

CAPTAIN PHILIP PIETERSE SCHUYLER.—[1600-1684]—New York Provincial Forces, 1667.

REFERENCE: Society of Colonial Wars Year Book, 1894, pp. 80, 85, 101, etc.

4. William Ruggles Tucker.

CAPTAIN PAUL SEARS.—[1637-1707]—Captain in the Mass. Militia, and served in the Narragansett War.

REFERENCE: Society of Colonial Wars Year Book, 1895, p. 272.

61. Victor Clifton Alderson.

RICHARD SEARS.—Was a member of Capt. William Palmer's Company at Yarmouth, Mass., Aug., 1643; was Representative to General Court at Plymouth, 1662.

REFERENCE: Pierce's Colonial Lists, 109-74; Society of Colonial Wars Year Book, 1895.

37. Frank Bassett Tobey.
61. Victor Clifton Alderson.

MAJOR GENERAL ROBERT SEDGWICK.—[1613-1656]—Captain of Charlestown, Mass., Company, 1636; Charter Member and Captain of Ancient and Honorable Artillery Company; Commander of Castle, 1641; member of the Colonial Council of War, 1643; Major General of the Mass. forces, 1652, in the expedition against Arcadia, and also in 1656 in the expedition against Jamaica.

REFERENCE: Society of Colonial Wars Year Book, 1895, p. 273.

43. Harry Linn Wright.

CAPTAIN RICHARD SEYMOUR.—Of Hartford and Farmington, Conn.; Captain of the Seymour Fort at Kensington.
REFERENCE: Andrews' History of New Britain, Conn., p. 19; Camp's History of New Britain, Conn., p. 28.
    1. Seymour Morris.

LIEUTENANT STEPHEN SEYMOUR.—Of Waterbury, Conn.; appointed Ensign of the train band in the Northbury Parish, in Waterbury, May, 1764; Lieutenant, May, 1765.
REFERENCE: Connecticut Colonial Records, pp. 253 and 349.
    1. Seymour Morris.

JOHN SHERMAN.—Of Watertown, Mass., was Ensign in 1654; Captain, 1680; Deputy, 1651-53-68.
REFERENCE: Society of Colonial Wars Year Book, 1895, p. 274.
    14. Henry Sherman Boutell.

JAMES SINCLAIR.—[1660-1731]—A soldier in King Philip's War. Was paid for service at Newbury, Mass., £2 18s. 6d. in defense of Block House.
REFERENCE: Bodge's Soldiers in King Philip's War.
    39. George Samuel Marsh.

REV. SAMUEL SKELTON.—Appointed member of the Governor Endicott's Council. First Pastor of the First Church of the Puritans in America.
REFERENCE: Savage's Genealogical Dictionary; Mass. Colonial Records, Vol. 1, pp. 387, 395, 361, 57.
    39. George Samuel Marsh.

JAMES SKIFF.—Was member of Lieut. John Blackmer's Co. at Sandwich, Mass., Aug., 1643.
REFERENCE: Pierce's Colonial Lists, p. 73.
    4. William Ruggles Tucker.
    37. Frank Bassett Tobey.

CORNELIUS BARENTSEN SLEGHT.—One of the nine original settlers of Kingston, N. Y. Sergeant of Military Company which built the Esopus stockade against the Indians by direction of Director General Peter Stuyvesant, and member of first board of Schepens, 1661. At Indian attack on Wiltwyck, June 7, 1663, Sleght was one of "the few men within the town by whom the savages, through God's mercy, were chased and put to flight," but carrying off with them over twenty women and children captives, among them a daughter of Sleght, who was forced to marry an Indian Warrior.
REFERENCE: Schoonmaker's History of New York, pp. 8, 13, 28, 30, 51 and fol. Documentary History of New York, Vol. IV, p. 29.
    13. Samuel Eberly Gross.

EDWARD SMITH.—Was Sergeant, 1662; Deputy to General Court of Rhode Island, 1665-8-75-76, 80-2-3; he was Assistant, 1691.

REFERENCE: Austin's Gen. Dictionary of R. I.; Rhode Island Colonial Records, Vol. 2, pp. 130, 139, 147.

75. Warren Lippitt Beckwith.

JOHN SMITH.—Afterwards Reverend, was member of Lieut. Thomas Dimmock's Company at Barnstable, Mass., Aug., 1643.

REFERENCE: Pierce's Colonial Lists, p. 73.

37. Frank Bassett Tobey.

NEHEMIAH SMITH.—Was Ensign at New London, Conn., 1697. Was Governor's Councillor, 1703; Deputy many years.

REFERENCE: Connecticut Colonial Records, 1689-1706, p. 212.

10. Edward Milton Adams.
51. Franklin Adams Meacham.

MARK SNOW.—Of Eastham, Mass., was member of town "War Council" appointed Feb. 29, 1675, for Eastham; this town "War Council" had control of garrisons, etc.

REFERENCE: Pierce's Colonial Lists, pp. 97-98.

50. Albert Eugene Snow.

NICHOLAS SNOW.—1676—Of Plymouth and Eastham. Member of Plymouth Military Company, 1643; Deputy from Eastham, 1648-50 and 1662.

REFERENCE: Pierce's Plymouth Colony Civil & Mil. Lists, p. 76; Plymouth Colony Records.

15. Josiah Lewis Lombard.
18. Scott Jordan.
50. Albert Eugene Snow.
58. Frederick La Forrest Merrick.

GEORGE SOULE.—[D. 1680]—One of the signers of the compact on Mayflower, 1620; Private in Lieut. Wm. Holmes' Company against Pequot Indians, 1637; Representative to the General Court from Duxbury, 1645-46-50-51-54.

REFERENCE: Plymouth Colony Records, Vol. 1; History of Plymouth Co., p. 364.

46. George Butters.

GENERAL CONSTANT SOUTHWORTH.—[1615-1697]—Served in the Pequot War, 1637; Ensign Duxbury Company, 1646; Lieutenant, 1653; Deputy from 1647 for twenty-two years; Treasurer of Plymouth Colony sixteen years; Member of the Council of War, 1658; Commissioner for the United Colonies, 1668, Commissary General during King Philip's War; Governor of Kennebec.

REFERENCE: Society of Colonial Wars Year Book, 1895, p. 276.

15. Josiah Lewis Lombard.
63. Rev. Abbott Eliot Kittredge.

JONATHAN SPARROW.—Of Eastham, Mass. Representative, 1668, and for eighteen years after; was called Lieutenant, 1676, and Captain, 1677, in town and Colonial records; was one of town "War Council," appointed Feb. 29, 1675; was Lieutenant under Capt. John Gorham at the Swamp Fight, Dec. 19, 1675; commissioned Oct. 4, 1675; was commissioned Captain of Eastham June, 1680; was member of Colonial "War Council" in King William's War, appointed Aug. 14, 1689; was one of a commission to adjust the expenses of this war; Dec. 25, 1689.

REFERENCE: Pierce's Colonial Lists, pp. 7, 10, 68, 95, 97, 98, 104.

50. Albert Eugene Snow.
61. Victor Clifton Alderson.

ENSIGN JARED SPENCER.—[1614-1685]—Cambridge and Lynn, Mass., and Haddam, Conn. Ensign of the Raddam Military Company during King Philip's War and after; Representative to the General Court for Haddam from 1674 to 1683.

REFERENCE: Savage's Gen. Dict. of New England; Connecticut Colonial Records, Vol. II, pp. 236, 261 and 365; Vol. III, pp. 3, 17, 26, 35, 48, 115, 121; Year Book Society Colonial Wars, 1895.

68. Albert Judson Fisher.

WILLIAM SPENCER.—Of Cambridge, Mass., and Hartford, Conn. Representative from Cambridge, Mass., to General Court, 1634-1638; Lieutenant of Militia; one of the founders of the Ancient and Honorable Artillery; Deputy to the General Court of Connecticut, 1639.

REFERENCE: Savage's Gen. Dict.

72. Lester Orestes Goddard.

CAPTAIN JOHN SPRAGUE.—Of Charlestown, Mass. [1624-1692]—Captain of the Massachusetts forces; Deputy to the General Court, 1692.

REFERENCE: Wyman's Charlestown Genealogies; Society of Colonial Wars Year Book.

5. John Smith Sargent.

JONATHAN SPRAGUE.—Soldier in Captain Maudsley's Company.

REFERENCE: Wyman's Charlestown Genealogies; Greens Book, Malden, Mass., p. 215.

5. John Smith Sargent.

RALPH SPRAGUE.—[1637]—Representative to the General Court for nine years. Member of the A. & H. Artillery Company, 1637. Lieutenant of same, 1639.

REFERENCE: Lickford's Note Book, p. 36; Wyman's Charlestown Genealogies.

5. John Smith Sargent.

MYLES STANDISH.—[1584-1656]—February 21, 1621, he received the first military commission given in this country. In 1649 he was appointed "General in Chief" of all the companies in the Colonies.

REFERENCE: Year Book of the Society of Colonial Wars, 1894, pp. 107, 115 and 177. Records of Plymouth Colony; "Ancient Landmarks of Plymouth"; Bancroft History of the U. S., Vol. 1, p. 209; History of Duxbury, Mass.

46. George Butters.

THOMAS STANTON.—Of Hartford and Stonington, Conn. Soldier in Pequot War, 1637. Interpreter later; served in the campaign of 1637 against the Pequot Indians; was appointed Marshal, 1638; was long in charge of negotiations with Indians, being versed in their language; was Deputy from Stonington, Conn., 1666, to Connecticut legislature.

REFERENCE: Society of Colonial Wars Year Book, 1894, p. 193; Connecticut Colonial Records, 1636-78.

10. Edward Milton Adams.
51. Franklin Adams Meacham.

SAMUEL STEARNS, JR.—[1713-1793]—Of Amherst, Mass., and Hollis, N. H. A private in Col. Blanchard's Regiment, 1754. Posted on the Connecticut River, Aug. 23, 1754.

REFERENCE: N. H. State papers, Vol. 3.

39. George Samuel Marsh.

SHUABEL STEARNS.—[1655-1734]—Of Cambridge and Lynnfield, Mass. Soldier in King Philip's War.

REFERENCE: Soldiers in King Philip's War, by Bodge.

39. George Samuel Marsh.

LIEUTENANT THOMAS STEBBINS.—Lieutenant in Captain Turner's Company at the Falls Fight in King Philip's War, May 19, 1676.

REFERENCE: Colonial Wars Year Book, 1895.

42. Charles Thomson Atkinson.

LIEUTENANT JOHN STEDMAN.—Wethersfield and Hartford, Conn. Commanded the Dragoons in the early part of King Philip's War, but died in Dec., 1675.

REFERENCE: Savage's Gene. Dictionary; Bodge's Soldiers in King Philip's War.

68. Albert Judson Fisher.

FRANCIS STILES.—Was commissioned Lieutenant of South Company at Woodbury, Conn., on May 10, 1773.

REFERENCE: Stiles' History of Windsor, Conn.; Connecticut Colonial Records, 1726-35, p. 431.

52. Hobart Chatfield Chatfield-Taylor.

EBENEZER STONE.—[1670-1754]—Of Newton, Mass. Deputy to the General Court of Massachusetts, 1708-1717. Subsequently Royal Councillor of the Province of Massachusetts.

REFERENCE: Society of Colonial Wars Year Book, 1895, p. 230.

6. Lyman Dresser Hammond.

SAMUEL STONE.—Of Cambridge, Mass., and Lexington, was a member of Capt. Thomas Prentiss' Company of Troopers. He was wounded at the great Swamp Fight at Kingston, R. I., on Dec. 19, 1675. On his recovery he served again in Capt. Thos. Brattle's Troop of Horse on an expedition to Mt. Hope, in Sept., 1676.

REFERENCE: N. E. Hist. & Gen. Reg., Vol. 37, pp. 231-232; Vol. 41, p. 273.

62. William Dorrance Messinger.

REV SAMUEL STONE.—Chaplain under Major John Mason in the Pequot War.

REFERENCE: Year Book of the Society of Colonial Wars, 1894, p. 84; Savage's Genealogical Dictionary, Vol. IV, p. 208; Connecticut Colonial Records of 1663, p. 413.

43. Harry Linn Wright.

JOHN STRATTON.—Was in Major Appleton's command in Narragansett Campaign of 1675-6.

REFERENCE: Mass. Archives, Vol. 68, p. 97; N. E. Hist. & Gen. Reg., Vol. 38, p. 443.

52. Hobart Chatfield Chatfield-Taylor.

SOCIETY OF COLONIAL WARS 157

THOMAS STRONG.—His enrollment and services in a troop of thirty-five (the first raised in the Colony of Connecticut) mustered at Windsor on March 11, 1657-8, for the protection of the Colony. This troop was commanded by Captain Richard Lord and was included in two forces under the command of Major John Mason.

REFERENCE: Records of the proceedings of the Connecticut Colonial Legislature (Trumbull's Edition) 1856, p. 309; Stiles' History of Windsor, Conn.

52. Hobart Chatfield Chatfield-Taylor.

JOHN STRONG.—[1707-1793]—Was a drummer in Capt. Benj. Allyn's Company from Windsor, Conn., in the Crown Point Expedition, Aug., 1755. Ensign in Gen. Phineas Seymour's command, Siege of Montreal.

REFERENCE: Stiles' History of Windsor, Vol. 1, pp. 251, 259; Conn. War Archives, Vol. 6.

21. William Wolcott Strong.

WILLIAM SUMNER.—[1605-1688]—Clerk of Train Band, Enfield, Conn.

REFERENCE: Records of Descendants of William Sumner of Dorchester, Mass., p. 2.

21. William Wolcott Strong.

WILLIAM SWIFT.—Was member of Lieut. John Blackmer's Co. at Sandwich, Mass., Aug., 1643.

REFERENCE: Pierce's Colonial Lists, p. 73

37. Frank Bassett Tobey.

DEPUTY GOVERNOR SAMUEL SYMONDS.—[1595-1678]—Ipswich, Mass. Deputy to the General Court, 1638-43. Assistant, 1643-73. Deputy Governor, 1673-78.

REFERENCE: Society of Colonial Wars Year Book, 1895, p. 281.

54. William Ward Wight.

ROBERT TAFT.—Was Captain of Mass. Colonial forces at Mendon, 1735, and later; was Representative many years.

REFERENCE: Society of Colonial Wars Year Book, 1894; Annals of Mendon (Metcalf) pp. 227, 236, 238, 244, 247.

10. Edward Milton Adams.
51. Franklin Adams Meacham.

ASA TAYLOR, SR.—Of Narragansett, (now Westminster, Mass.) was private in Capt. Asa Whitcomb's Co. of Colonel Bagley's Regiment, raised about 1757 for the reduction of Canada; was in service March to December, 1758; was again recruited 1759.

REFERENCE: Heywood's History of Westminster, p. 102.

    52. Hobart Chatfield Chatfield-Taylor.

SURGEON OLIVER TEALL.—Was born in New Haven, Conn., studied medicine and surgery, removed to Killingworth, Conn., entered the English Army as a Surgeon, and served through the French War.

REFERENCE: Genealogical and Historical Notes of the Teall Family.

    7. Edward McKinstry Teall.

EPHRAIM TERRY.—[1701-1703]—Captain of Enfield Train Band, 1751.

REFERENCE: Connecticut Colonial Records, Vol. X, p. 53.

    21. William Wolcott Strong.

STEPHEN TERRY.—[1668]—Of Windsor, Conn., was a member of Capt. Lord's Company of "Troopers," the first body of horse raised in New England; was mustered in March 11, 1657.

REFERENCE: Savage's Genealogical Dictionary; Connecticut Colonial Records, Vol. 1636-1665, p. 309; S. C. W. Year Book, 1895, p. 283.

    10. Edward Milton Adams.
    43. Harry Linn Wright.
    52. Hobart Chatfield Chatfield-Taylor.

CAPTAIN SAMUEL THOMPSON.—Lieutenant, and later Captain of first Company New Haven Train Band; Deputy to General Assembly, 1716.

REFERENCE: Colonial Records of Connecticut, 1703-1716, p. 143, 394, 546.

    42. Charles Thomson Atkinson.

JOHN THURSTON.—Of Dedham, Mass. Served against the Indians 1675-6.

REFERENCE: N. E. Historical & Gen. Register, Vol. 43, p. 272.

    10. Edward Milton Adams.
    40. Frank Eugene Spooner.
    51. Franklin Adams Meacham.

LIEUTENANT THOMAS THURSTON.—In 1675 was a Sergeant, promoted to Lieutenant in 1678, doing good service in King Philip's War. In 1676 he represented Medfield, Mass., in the General Court of Mass.

REFERENCE: Thurston Family Genealogy; History of Medfield.

70. Charles Ridgely.

THOMAS TOBEY, SR.—Was a member of Council of War for town of Sandwich, Mass. Appointed Feb. 29, 1676. [He was granted fifty to sixty acres of land July 7, 1681, for services in King Philip's War.] At a Council of War held at Marshfield, Feb. 29, 1676, Thomas Tobey, Sr., was appointed one of council for town and other military forces at that town, could enroll and impress men, etc.

REFERENCE: Freeman's History of Cape Cod, Vol. 1, p. 285; Vol. 1, p. 295; Plymouth Colony Records, Vol. 6, pp. 66; Vol. V, p. 196.

37. Frank Bassett Tobey.

CAPTAIN THOMAS TOPPING.—Captain of the Southampton, L. I., Militia, 1651; Assistant, 1655-8, 1659-63.

REFERENCE: Savage's Genealogical Dictionary, Vol. 4, pp. 255; Howell's History East Hampton, p. 32; Palfrey's New England, Vol. 2, p. 638.

25. Frank Baker.

LIEUTENANT JOHN TRACY.—Was Ensign of the Military Company at Duxbury, Mass., 1682; was appointed Lieutenant Oct. 2, 1689. Plymouth Colonial forces. Was Deputy to the General Court from Norwich, 1683-86.

REFERENCE: Pierce's Colonial Lists; Plymouth Colony Records, Vol. V, pp. 84 and 218.

10. Edward Milton Adams.
51. Franklin Adams Meacham.

SOLOMON TRACY.—Commissioned Ensign in 1698; Lieutenant, 1701; Deputy to General Court twelve sessions; in 1711 Clerk of the House; in 1717 Speaker of the House.

REFERENCE: Conn. Colonial Records, Vol. 3.

70. Charles Ridgely.

LIEUTENANT THOMAS TRACY.—[1610-1685]—Ensign First Train Band, Norwich, Conn., 1666; in 1672 Lieutenant of New London Co. Dragoons, enlisted to fight the Dutch and Indians. Member of the General Court twenty-seven sessions. Commissary in King Philip's War.

REFERENCE: Society of Colonial Wars Year Book, 1895, p. 285.

70. Charles Ridgely.
71. Ebenezer Lane.

RICHARD TREAT.—[1590-1669]—Of Wethersfield, Conn., 1669; Representative to the General Court and re-elected many times; Assistant Magistrate of the Colony, 1658-1665; named in the Royal Charter of Charles II. as one of the patentees for Connecticut, 1662.

REFERENCE: Society of Colonial Wars Year Book, 1894, p. 55; Year Book, 1895, p. 286.

1. Seymour Morris.
15. Josiah Lewis Lombard.
33. Deming Haven Preston.
43. Harry Linn Wright.
63. Rev. Abbott Eliot Kittredge.

GOVERNOR ROBERT TREAT.—[1622-1710]—Commander at Great Swamp Fight; Major commanding Connecticut Troops at the Battles of Hadley and Springfield; Deputy Governor, 1676-86; appointed Governor, 1686; resigned, 1701; in the encounter with the Indians at Bloody Brook, Sept. 18, 1675, his arrival on the scene of action with the Connecticut forces turned the tide.

REFERENCE: Society of Colonial Wars Year Book, 1895, p. 286.

15. Josiah Lewis Lombard.
63. Rev. Abbott Eliot Kittredge.

LIEUTENANT JAMES TROWBRIDGE.—[1636-1717]—Of Newton, Mass. Deputy to the General Court from Cambridge, 1700-1703. Served in King Philip's War.

REFERENCE: Society of Colonial Wars Year Book, 1895, p. 296.

6. Lyman Dresser Hammond.

CAPTAIN MOSES TUCKER.—Of New Ipswich, N. H. His house was fortified and used as a garrison for the neighborhood during the Indian raid on the town. He was a Captain in the French and Indian War.

REFERENCE: N. H. Archives; History of Ipswich, N. H., p. 437.

4. William Ruggles Tucker.

NATHANIEL TURNER.—Captain, ——, 1647. Captain in Pequot War; Assistant, 1639.

REFERENCE: Savage's Gen. Dictionary.

43. Harry Linn Wright.

SAMUEL UFFORD.—Was appointed Ensign of Stratford, Conn., May 13, 1714; promoted Lieutenant May 12, 1720.

REFERENCE: Connecticut Colonial Records, 1706-1716, p. 429; Vol. 1717-1725, p. 175.

59. Charles Pratt Whitney.

LIEUTENANT PHINEAS UPHAM.—Entered service about September, 1675, under Captain Isaac Johnson, and took part with his company, Dec. 19, 1675, in the storming of Fort Cononicus, or the battle of the Great Swamp Fort. Capt. Johnson being killed in this battle, Lieut. Upham succeeded him in command and was himself severely wounded.

REFERENCE: Military Records, Vol. 1, 280; also page 276; Mass. Archives, Vol. 68, p. 104; Year Book Society of Colonial Wars, 1894, pp. 31 and 208.

29. Frederic William Upham.
55. Gov. William Henry Upham.

OLOFF STEVENSON VAN CORTLANDT.—[1600-1684]— In 1649, Colonel of the "City Train Band," and in 1655-1664, the last Burgomaster of New Amsterdam, under the Dutch, before the English conquest.

REFERENCE: Society of Colonial Wars Year Book, 1894, pp. 29, 34, 55, etc.

4. William Ruggles Tucker.

COLONEL STEPHANES VAN CORTLANDT.—[1643-1710] —Kings County Regiment, 1671-1693; Mayor of New York City, 1677; Member of King's Council, 1680-1700.

REFERENCE: Society of Colonial Wars Year Book, 1894, pp. 45, 91, 97, etc.

4. William Ruggles Tucker.

LIEUTENANT GOVERNOR GEORGE VAUGHAN.—[1676-1725]—Colonel of Provincial Forces during Queen Anne's War; elected by General Assembly, 1707; Representative of Province to England; appointed Lieutenant Governor of the Province, commission dated July 18, 1715; resigned Sept. 30, 1717.

REFERENCE: History of Cutt family, p. 503.

46. George Butters.

WILLIAM VAUGHAN.—[1640-1719]—In 1672 was Lieutenant of Cavalry under Captain Robert Pike; Captain in 1680; in 1681 was promoted to Major, commanding the Militia of the Province.

REFERENCE: History of Cutt family, p. 489; Savage's Genealogical Dictionary, Adjutant Gen. Reports of N. H.

46. George Butters.

JONATHAN WADE.—Called Major and Captain. Captain of the Three County Troops of Horse.

REFERENCE: Savage's Genealogical Dictionary, p. 378; History of Medford, Mass.; N. E. Hist. & Gen. Register, Vol. XLIII, p. 274; Soldiers in King Philip's War

5. John Smith Sargent.

CAPTAIN JOHN WADSWORTH.—Was a Lieutenant and Captain in King Philip's War. A Representative in the General Assembly from Hartford. On Oct. 31, 1687, he secreted the charter of Connecticut, granted by Charles II. in 1662, in an oak tree in Hartford, on Wyllys Hill, to prevent the same being taken by Sir Edmund Andros, who came to Hartford with sixty men to wrest it by force from the Colonists.

REFERENCE: Trumbull's History Connecticut, Vol. 1, p. 391; Savage's Genealogical Dictionary, Vol. 4, p. 380; Wadsworth Family in America, p. 85; Year Book, 1894, Society of Colonial Wars, p. 197.

43. Harry Linn Wright.

BENJAMIN WAIT.—Of Hatfield, Mass., was Sergeant; killed by Indians at Deerfield, Mass., Feb. 29, 1704.

REFERENCE: Savage's Gen. Dict.; Judd's History of Hadley, Mass.

60. John Conant Long.

JOSEPH WAIT.—Enlisted May, 1754, in Captain Eleazer Melvin's Company. In December, 1754, Corporal in John Burk's Company of Rangers, and was stationed at Falltown. He served in the expedition to Crown Point and in Colonel Ephraim William's Regiment in the Battle of Lake George, Sept. 8, 1755, and became an Ensign in this Regiment when commanded by Seth Pomeroy, after the death of Colonel Williams. In the winter of 1756 he served at Fort Edward and Fort William Henry when the Regiment was commanded by Colonel Joseph Dwight; was transferred to Major Robert Roger's corps of Rangers in January, 1757; participated in the fight at "Roger's Slide," Lake George.

REFERENCE: Published Journal of Major Robert Rogers; Society of Colonial Wars Year Book, 1895, p. 11.

26. Horatio Loomis Wait.

MAJOR RICHARD WALDRON.—[1616-1689]—Representative to the General Court, 1651-57-61; was one of Council under new form of government of New Hampshire, 1680; on death of President Cutt, 1681, was head of the Province until arrival of Royal Governor. He was Captain in early days and Major in the Indian War, 1675-6. He was killed by the Indians.

REFERENCE: Savage's Dictionary; Adjutant Gen. Reports, N. H.

46. George Butters.

JOHN WARD.—His house was built by him for and used as a garrison during King Philip's War, 1675.

REFERENCE: Society of Colonial Wars Year Book, 1895, p. 292.

31. Charles Newton Fessenden.

WILLIAM WARD.—In garrison at Sudbury, Mass., in King Philip's War.

REFERENCE: Society of Colonial Wars Year Book, 1895, p. 292.

31. Charles Newton Fessenden.

CAPTAIN JOSEPH WARNER.—Of Hardwick, Mass. Captain in the French War. Commanded a Company that marched for the relief of Fort William Henry, August 9, 1757.

REFERENCE: History of Hardwick.

72. Lester Orestes Goddard.

DANIEL WARREN.—Of Watertown, Mass. A soldier in King Philip's War.

REFERENCE: Society of Colonial Wars Year Book, 1895, p. 293; N. E. Hist. & Gen. Register, Vol. 43, p. 279.

4. William Ruggles Tucker.
67. John Demmon Vandercook.

JAMES WARRINER.—[1641-1727]—Springfield, Mass., Aug. 19, 1668, he was sent as a soldier by Col. Pynchon to the relief of Quabang (Brookfield). He was again sent by Col. Pynchon on Sept. 21, 1688, under command of Henry Gilbert, to scout for Indians about Brookfield and to make fortifications there. They built the Gilbert Fort, which served Brookfield in future wars.

REFERENCE: Savage's Genealogical Dict.; History of Springfield, by M. A. Greene, pp. 194-262; "West Springfield Centennial," p. 97; History of North Brookfield, pp. 140, 141 and 153.

68. Albert Judson Fisher.

JOHN WASHBURN.—Of Duxbury, Mass., 1645 was in an expedition fitted out that year against the Narragansetts and their confederates; and the town of Duxbury furnished six men "wch went wth those that went first," and "were forth XVII dayes."

REFERENCE: Winsor's History of Duxbury, Mass.; Plymouth Colony Records, Vol. II, p. 90.

34. Hempstead Washburne.

DAVID WATERBURY.—Was appointed Ensign of Fairchild Co. Dragoons, April, 1690; was appointed Lieutenant of Stamford Train Band 1698; he served in King Philip's War, 1675-6.

REFERENCE: Connecticut Colonial Records, Vol. 10, pp. 21. 253; Huntington's History of Stamford, pp. 113-14.

10. Edward Milton Adams.

LAWRENCE WATERS.—[1687]—A soldier in the garrison at Lancaster, 1675, and earlier. One of the three first settlers of Lancaster, Mass. Soldiers in King Philip's War, East side of North River.

REFERENCE: Society Colonial Wars Year Book, 1895, p. 293; Marvin's "History of Lancaster," pp. 61 and 110; Nourse's "Early Records of Lancaster," pp. 128, 133, 139.

    4. William Ruggles Tucker.
  18. Scott Jordan.
  26. Horatio Loomis Wait.
  67. John Demmon Vandercook.
  68. Albert Judson Fisher.

GOVERNOR JOHN WEBSTER.—[——1661]—Hartford, 1636; Representative, 1637; Magistrate, 1639 to 1655; Deputy Gov. of Connecticut, 1655; Governor of Connecticut, 1656; one of the commissioners of the United Colonies.

REFERENCE: Savage's Dictionary; Society of Colonial Wars Year Book, 1895, p. 293.

  43. Harry Linn Wright.

ROBERT WEBSTER.—[——1676]—Lieutenant, 1654; in service in war of 1675.

REFERENCE: Savage's Genealogical Dictionary.

  43. Harry Linn Wright.

GOVERNOR THOMAS WELLS.—[1598-1660]—Of Wethersfield, Conn.; Magistrate of Governing Court, 1637-60; Second Treasurer, 1639-51; Secretary, 1640-48; Governor (pro tem.) 1651; Deputy Governor, 1654-56-57-59; Governor, 1655-58; Commissioner for United Colonies, 1649.

REFERENCE: Society of Colonial Wars Year Book, 1895, p. 294.

  69. Samuel Rogers Wells.

WILLIAM WESTWOOD.—[1606-1669]—One of the commissioners appointed by Mass. Bay Colony to govern the Colony of Connecticut, 1636; Assistant Connecticut Colony, 1637.

REFERENCE: Society Colonial Wars Year Book, 1895, p. 295.

  42. Charles Thomson Atkinson.
  43. Harry Linn Wright.
  45. Francis Porter Fisher.

CHRISTOPHER WHEATON.—Soldier in King Philip's War, under Capt. Isaac Johnson and Captain John Jacob, March 24, 1675.

REFERENCE: N. E. Hist. & Gen. Register, Vol. XXXIX, pp. 76-78; History of Hingham, 1894-5; Converse Genealogy, 1892-3.

  5. John Smith Sargent.

SOCIETY OF COLONIAL WARS

JOHN WHEELER.—Of Concord, 1642; served in Captain Davenport's Company in Great Swamp Fight.

REFERENCE: New England Historical and Genealogical Register, Vol. 39, pp. 258 and 261.

25. Frank Baker.

LIEUTENANT JOSEPH WHEELER.—Lieutenant of the Concord Militia in King Philip's War.

REFERENCE: New England Historical and Genealogical Register, Vol. 43, p. 276.

24. Lemuel Ruggles Hall.

SERGEANT THOMAS WHEELER.—[1628-1704]—Sergeant in Captain Timothy Wheeler's Company of Concord, Mass., and under Major Willard.

REFERENCE: Shattuck's Concord, p. 46; New England Historical and Genealogical Register, Vol. 37, p. 84; Vol. 38, p. 224.

25. Frank Baker.

CAPTAIN TIMOTHY WHEELER.—[1697-1782]—A member of Concord, Mass., Militia.

REFERENCE: Concord Records, p. 432.

25. Frank Baker.

TIMOTHY WHEELER.—Captain from Concord, Mass.; served in King Philip's War; Deputy nine years from 1663.

REFERENCE: Society of Colonial Wars Year Book, 1895, p. 295.

14. Henry Sherman Boutell.

JOHN WHIPPLE.—Was Deputy from Providence to the General Court, 1666. He was at that time called Captain in the Colonial Records.

REFERENCE: R. I. Colonial Records, Vol. 2 (1664-77) p. 150.

75. Warren Lippitt Beckwith.

CAPTAIN JOHN WHIPPLE.—[1626-1683]—Lieutenant in Capt. John Appleton's Troop, 1668. Lieutenant of Capt. Nicholas Paige's Company in the first, or Mount Hope Campaign. King Philip's War, 1675. Captain of Spanish Troop in 1676. Deputy to General Court, 1674-79-82-83.

REFERENCE: Society of Colonial Wars Year Book. 1895, p. 295.

14. Henry Sherman Boutell.
73. Anthony French Merrill.

JOSEPH WHIPPLE.—Was Deputy or Representative to the General Court of Rhode Island nineteen years, during the period 1698-1728; he was Assistant, 1714; Colonel of the land forces, 1719-20; was called Captain, 1722.

REFERENCE: Austin's Gen. Dictionary of R. I., pp. 223; R. I. Colonial Records, Vol. 4, pp. 309, 169, 267, 324.

75. Warren Lippitt Beckwith.

JOHN WHITCOMB.—Of Dorchester, Scituate and Lancaster, Mass. In August, 1643, a member of Military Company of Scituate.

REFERENCE: Pierce's Colonial Lists, p. 74.

4. William Ruggles Tucker.
26. Horatio Loomis Wait.
67. John Demmon Vandercook.

REV. JOHN WHITING.—[—— 1689]—Was Chaplain of Hartford forces in King Philip's War.

REFERENCE: Society of Colonial Wars Year Book, 1895.

45. Francis Porter Fisher.

WILLIAM WHITING.—[—— 1647]—Elected to Court of Magistrates, 1637; Treasurer of Connecticut Colony, 1641-1647; chosen Major, 1642.

REFERENCE: Colonial Records of Connecticut, Vol. 1, p. 496; Trumbull's History of Hartford Co., Vol. 1, p. 269; Savage's Gen. Dict., Vol. 4, p. 521.

21. William Wolcott Strong.

FRANCIS WHITMORE.—[1625-1685]—Of Cambridge. Served in Indian wars under Major Simon Willard.

REFERENCE: Society of Colonial Wars Year Book, 1895, p. 296.

18. Scott Jordan.
62. William Dorrance Messinger.

ENSIGN THOMAS WHITMORE.—[1673-1752]—Of Cambridge, Mass., and Killingly, Conn. May, 1742, commissioned Ensign of the Third Company or Train Band of Killingly. Deputy from Killingly to General Assembly, 1720-25 and 1729.

REFERENCE: Connecticut Colonial Records, Vol. 8, p. 449.

18. Scott Jordan.

JOHN WHITNEY.—[1624-1692]—A member of Capt. Hugh Mason's Company of Watertown, Mass. Enrolled in 1675. Served in the Sudbury fight, April 29, 1676.

REFERENCE: Massachusetts Archives, Vol. 68, p. 74; Forbush Genealogy; Bond's History of Watertown; Society of Colonial Wars Year Book, 1895, p. 296; Pierce's Whitney Genealogy, pp. 22 and 24.

17. Frederick Clifton Pierce.
18. Scott Jordan.
26. Horatio Loomis Wait.
45. Francis Porter Fisher.
49. Frank Eugene Spooner.
59. Charles Pratt Whitney.

SERGEANT SAMUEL WILBOUR.—Of Portsmouth, R. I. Chosen Clerk of the Train Band, June 27, 1638; appointed Sergeant, 1644.

REFERENCE: Austin's Genealogical Dictionary of R. I.

4. William Ruggles Tucker.

GEORGE WILLARD.—A member of the "Scituate Company" of Plymouth Colony; active service, 1643-4.

REFERENCE: Society of Colonial Wars Year Book, 1895, p. 297.

61. Victor Clifton Alderson.

MAJOR SIMON WILLARD.—[1605-1676]—Founder of Concord, Mass., 1630. He was Deputy, 1630 to 1649. Assistant, 1651 and held that office until the time of his death. Commissioned Lieutenant Commandant March, 1637, in the Train Band; promoted Captain of the Colonial forces, 1646, and again Sergeant Major in command of the Middlesex regiment in 1653, and held same for 23 years. Was Commander in Chief against the Niantics in 1654. Commanded the Middlesex regiment of Massachusetts Troops in King Philip's War. Led the relief at the battle of Brookfield, August, 1675. Fought, defeated and dispersed the Indians who had attacked Groton, March 17, 1676.

REFERENCE: History of Concord, Mass.; History of Chelmsford, Mass.; Colonial Records of Massachusetts, pp. 122, 152, 180, 181, 187, 194, 210 and 214; Year Book, General Society of Colonial Wars.

2. Captain Philip Reade.
26. Horatio Loomis Wait.

ISAAC WILLIAMS.—Was commissioned Lieutenant at Cambridge May 26, 1647.

REFERENCE: Mass. Col. Records, Vol. 5, p. 173

52. Hobart Chatfield Chatfield-Taylor.

SERGEANT JOHN WILSON.—[—— 1687]—Of Woburn, Mass. Soldier from June, 1675, to August, 1667. He was with Capt. Samuel Mosely in 1675, and was at Mount Hope, Aug. 9, 1675. Soldier under Capt. Richard Beers of Watertown, Mass., Jan. 25, 1676. Was under Capt. Samuel Brocklebank of Rowley, Mass. Soldier in Capt. John Cutler's Company of Charlestown, Mass., after the Sudbury disaster, King Philip's War

REFERENCE: Soldiers of King Philip's War, Bodge, pp. 21, 87, 159, 241, 315.

2. Captain Philip Reade.

SERGEANT SAMUEL WILSON.—[1658-1729]—Of Woburn, Mass., was a Corporal, 1694; Sergeant, 1695-1729, in the local military company of Militia or Train Band, being continuously in the military service from the age of 36 to 71.

REFERENCE: Savage's Genealogical Dictionary, Vol. IV, p. 588; History of Middlesex Co., p. 387; History of Woburn, p. 649.

2. Captain Philip Reade.

LIEUTENANT EDWARD WINSHIP.—Ensign and Lieutenant, 1660; member of the Ancient and Honorable Artillery Company, 1638.

REFERENCE: Society of Colonial Wars Year Book, 1895, p. 299.

14. Henry Sherman Boutell.
31. Charles Newton Fessenden.

ISAAC WINSHIP.—Private in Capt. Benjamin Reed's Company of Lexington, Mass., 1759, and in Capt. Wm. Reed's Company of Lexington, Mass., in 1755.

REFERENCE: Mass. Archives, Vol. 97, p. 216; Hudson's History of Lexington, Mass., p. 378.

31. Charles Newton Fessenden.

LIEUTENANT JOB WINSLOW.—Was in command of the Train Band at Freetown, Mass., in 1702, and served in the fight at Swansea, Mass., in 1675.

REFERENCE: Society of Colonial Wars Year Book, 1895, p. 299.

67. John Demmon Vandercook.

MAJOR GENERAL ROGER WOLCOTT.—[1679-1767]—Major General and second in command at siege of Louisbourg, 1745. Governor of Connecticut, 1751-1754; 1709 chosen Representative for that town in the General Assembly; 1711 went in the expedition against Canada, Commissary of the Connecticut Stores; 1714 was chosen a member of the Council; 1741 chosen Deputy Governor of this Colony; 1745 led forth the Connecticut troops on the expedition against Cape Breton and received a commission from Governor Shirley and General Law for Major General of the Army.

REFERENCE: Society of Colonial Wars Year Book, 1895, p. 200. Notes from family manuscripts in possession of Ebenezer Lane.

21. William Wolcott Strong.
71. Ebenezer Lane.

REV. JOHN WOODBRIDGE.—Was a member of Ancient and Honorable Military Co., Boston, 1644. Was Assistant.

REFERENCE: Savage's Gen. Dict.; Whitmore's Artillery Company; Mass. Colonial Records.

4. William Ruggles Tucker.
10. Edward Milton Adams.
24. Lemuel Ruggles Hall.

LIEUTENANT EDWARD WOODMAN.—Lieutenant, 1637; served in Pequot War.

REFERENCE: Society of Colonial Wars Year Book, p. 300.

31. Charles Newton Fessenden.

GEORGE WOODWARD.—Of Watertown, was private in Capt. John Cutter's Company and died while his name was still on the roll, May 31, 1676.

REFERENCE: N. E. Historical & Gen. Reg., Vol. 42, p. 299.

62. William Dorrance Messinger.

CAPTAIN EDWARD WRIGHT.—Sudbury, Mass.; soldier in King Philip's War.

REFERENCE: Savage's Genealogical Dictionary.

25. Frank Baker.

JOHN WYETH.—Soldier in Capt. Gookin's Company, King Philip's War.

REFERENCE: Year Book General Society of Colonial Wars, 1895, p. 300.

31. Charles Newton Fessenden.

JOHN WYMAN.—Member of Capt. Prentiss' Company of 73 troopers in Middlefield. "A list of Major Sam. Appleton souldiers yt were slaine & wounded the 19th Decemb 75 at the Indians' fort at Narragansett; of Captaine Prentise his troopers slaine & wounded Jno. Wyman slaine."

REFERENCE: Massachusetts Archives, Vol. 68, p. 73; Vol. 68, p. 104.

22. Walter Channing Wyman.

LIEUTENANT JOHN WYMAN.—Lieutenant in Captain Thomas Prentiss' Company; fought at Mount Hope and the Narragansett campaign, and at last received a wound in the face. Registered in Capt. Prentiss' troops Aug. 27, 1675, to June 24, 1676.

REFERENCE: Massachusetts Archives, Vol. 68, p. 104; New England Historical & Genealogical Register, pp. 280, 281, 282.

22. Walter Channing Wyman.

www.ingramcontent.com/pod-product-compliance
Lightning Source LLC
Chambersburg PA
CBHW030746230426
43667CB00007B/861